D1376025

SPENSER'S
IMAGES OF LIFE

SPENSER'S
IMAGES OF LIFE

BY

C.S.LEWIS

EDITED BY ALASTAIR FOWLER

CAMBRIDGE
AT THE UNIVERSITY PRESS
1967

Published by the Syndics of the Cambridge University Press
Bentley House, 200 Euston Road, London, N.W. 1
American Branch: 32 East 57th Street, New York, N.Y. 10022

Library of Congress Catalogue Card Number: 67–21961

Printed in Great Britain
at the University Printing House, Cambridge
(Brooke Crutchley, University Printer)

CONTENTS

PREFACE

Most of the ideas and some of the words in this book are from C. S. Lewis's Cambridge lectures on Spenser. The holograph notes for these lectures are at present in the possession of the Rev. Walter Hooper, and a xerox copy has been deposited in the Bodleian Library (shelf-mark MS. Facs. d. 135). Lewis intended to use the material of the lectures for a book, but he did not live to do so. Only a few pages reached a further draft: these have already been printed without alteration in *Studies in Medieval and Renaissance Literature by C. S. Lewis*, ed. Walter Hooper (Cambridge, 1966), under the title 'Spenser's Cruel Cupid'. Their equivalent in the present volume will be found at pp. 18–26. Most of the lecture notes are in the form of a private *aide-mémoire*, so that when I was asked if I would prepare them for publication my first reaction was to reject the proposal as impracticable. In their original shape the notes were intelligible only with difficulty. On the other hand, they contained ideas too interesting to be delivered lightly to oblivion. I therefore decided (though not until I had taken the valued advice of Mr Wallace Robson) to engage in the invidious enterprise of expanding the notes and making a book of them myself.

I found that the task was not an invidious one at all, but a deep satisfaction. For it continued in an unexpected way the combative friendship I had come to enjoy with the author. Eventually I agreed with many of the opinions

in the notes, and, where I disagreed, I saw the weightiness
of his case. Consequently in the pages that follow the
reader will not be troubled with many footnotes express-
ing scrupulous reservations on the part of the editor.
Nor does my regard for Lewis allow room for the staking
of claims to originality. When the proportions of the
argument required it, I have freely and tacitly interpo-
lated developments of my own, or added such examples
as seemed germane. I have also tacitly corrected errors
of fact and of transcription, and supplied references to the
quotations. My aim throughout has been to make a
readable book. At the same time, I have tried to adhere
to Lewis's own thought wherever research or memory
could recover it. Similarly with his words, though of
course no attempt has been made to counterfeit his style.
The best the reader can expect is that from time to time
the book may be like Silenus: ugly and shaggy outside,
but wise within. And the best I hope for is that some may
agree with me that if Lewis himself had lived to write the
book it might have stood out among his works as a
critical new departure. Here I am not thinking of the
iconographical interpretations (although these have their
interest) so much as of the adumbration of a manner of
approach to fiction not suitable for textual analysis.

I wish to thank Lewis's executors, Major W. H. Lewis
and Mr Owen Barfield, for making the lecture notes
available to me. Professor J. L. Ackrill, Professor J. C.
Maxwell, Mr Philip Radcliffe and the Rev. L. M. Styler
helped to find references or to solve problems of
interpretation; and a particularly formidable debt is owed

to Dr Sydney Anglo, without whose generous assistance the reconstruction of the passages relating to pageants and tournaments would hardly have been possible.

Biblical quotations are given in the form of the Authorized (King James) Version, except that the Psalms are sometimes quoted from Coverdale's version. Spenser references are to the Oxford Standard Authors edition of *The Poetical Works of Edmund Spenser*, ed. J. C. Smith and E. de Selincourt (1912). If the place of publication is not given in a footnote reference it may be assumed to be London.

A. D. S. F.

Brasenose College,
Oxford

F. Q. perhaps the most difficult poem in English. After [40] years of reading I am just beginning to realise its difficulty.

Like most old lit. demands a double response for full enjoyment. Falstaff both a funny fat man and an ironic comment on the world he is in. Hamlet a profound exploration of Death and a rousing melodrama. The Comedia both a mimesis of the whole spiritual life and also first-class science fiction. Neither a prig nor a simpleton can fully appreciate any of them.

But little can get something out of them!

But in FQ the simplicity is not your kind of simplicity and the sophistication not your kind of sophistication.

The Simplicity: A.

Cowley. Of Myself. There was wont to lye in my mother's parlour Spenser's works. This I happened to fall upon and was infinitely delighted with the stories of the Knights and Giants and Monsters and brave Houses which I found everywhere.

(As long as Romanticism lasted the poem c. be enjoyed on this level alone. This is Hazlitt's, Keats's, Tennyson's FQ)

Sophistication: B A.

This sort of story complicated by the Polyphonic Technique. And because it is unfinished the interlacing is always often tangled.

Simplicity B

The "moral allegory" i.e. the story has a moral. S. George defeats Error, falls into Pride, is captured by despair, purged by Penance, raised by contemplation, and finally defeats the devil.

(This is Ruskin's FQ).

Sophistication B

E. K. on June (25) cites "An hundred graces on her eyelids sat" for S. Pageants. Almost the same b. (When her eyelids many graces sat) occurs FQ I. 3. 25.

Cf. II 1. 33 But you, fair Sir, whose pageant next succeeds.

Was FQ originally "Pageants"?

It is very very s. after a verbalisation of Pageant i.e. procession or

C. S. Lewis's manuscript, folio 1 (text pp. 1-3)

2. Contrasted with a real head of Chivalry

   a. B)(Radigund

   b. B–Artegall relation)(Radigund–Artegall relation.

a. There is nothing of the virago or feminist about B. She had become a knight errant only in order to find her lover.
Her outlook has always been wholly feminine

III 2. 23 Looks in the fallen magic mirror to see her future husband. Not because she's in love, or wanton, but "as maidens use to done" – as girls do. She "must her life at last must linke in that same knot

Radigund is the real Feminist.
She is revenging herself on all mankind because one man refused her love (V. 4. 30).
Her revenge takes the form of directly reversing the roles of the sexes: "For all those knights the which by force or guile, she doth subdue, she foully doth entreate. First she doth them of warlike armes despoile and clothe in womens weedes. And then with threat Doth them constrein to worke, to earne their meat, To spin, to card, to sew, to row, to wring. (31)

Yes? Yes. She is to S. both a horrible and a comic figure
Her attendant Amazons are "an uncouth sight" (21)
On first seeing A "Her heart for rage did grate and teeth did grin" (27)
Britomart "She raught her such an huge stroke that it of sense distraught her. And had she not it warded warily it had deprived her mother of a daughter (41).
Spite "And beare with you both wine and juncates fit And bad her eat; henceforth he oft shall hungry rise" (49).
b. First of all A. makes the harmation of agreeing to fight on the terms that the vanquished will be the others slave
Then follows the fight. V. like, yet v. unlike, his fight with B in IV 6.
2. Both A. slashes off his enemies helm & sees a womans face.
But:

INTRODUCTION

The Faerie Queene is perhaps the most difficult poem in English. Quite how difficult, I am only now beginning to realize after forty years of reading it. For one thing, it demands for its full enjoyment a double response. But in this, of course, it is like most old literature. Falstaff is both a funny fat man and an ironic comment on the world he inhabits; *Hamlet,* both a profound exploration of death and a rousing melodrama; the *Divina commedia,* both a mimesis of the whole spiritual life and first-class science fiction. Neither a prig nor a simpleton can fully appreciate any of these, but either can get something from all of them.

With Spenser, however, there are special complications. He, too, calls for both a simple and a sophisticated response. But the simplicity of *The Faerie Queene* is not our kind of simplicity, nor its sophistication our kind of sophistication. We are not much given, now, to reading it simply for the story, as Cowley tells us he was—

there was wont to lye in my Mothers Parlour ... *Spencers* Works; this I happened to fall upon, and was infinitely delighted with the Stories of the Knights, and Giants, and Monsters, and brave Houses, which I found every where there.[1]

As long as Romanticism lasted, the poem could be enjoyed on the narrative level alone. This was Hazlitt's *Faerie Queene,* and Keats's, and Tennyson's. But in our

[1] 'Of My Self', *Essays, Plays and Sundry Verses,* ed. A. R. Waller (Cambridge, 1906), 457.

day that simplicity of response has gone. On the other hand, this sort of romantic story used often to be very complicated formally. For it was customary in Spenser's time to use a polyphonic technique, interweaving different narrative strands in an intricate way. The enjoyment of the story in this sense—of the interplay of stories— could be a very sophisticated response indeed. But such a response is always difficult for us to make now. And in the case of *The Faerie Queene* it is particularly so, since the poem is unfinished, and the interlacing in consequence often bungled.

Again, Spenser's poem is simple in that it is a moral allegory. That is to say, its story has a moral. St George defeats error, falls into pride, is dominated by despair, purged by penance, and raised by contemplation, and finally defeats the devil. This is Ruskin's *Faerie Queene*; but it is not ours. We are unaccustomed to respond to a content so simple. Yet we are simpletons ourselves when it comes to responding to another element of *The Faerie Queene*, to which Spenser and his earlier readers paid the most discriminating attention. I mean the element of Pageant.

In his gloss on the phrase 'Many Graces', E. K. notes that 'thys same Poete [i.e. Spenser] in his Pageaunts sayth. An hundred Graces on her eyeledde satte.'[1] Yet almost the same line—'Upon her eyelids many Graces sate'—occurs in *The Faerie Queene* at II, iii, 25. This poses a question that

[1] Gloss on *Shepheardes Calender*, 'June', l. 25. E. K., who provided editorial comment on *The Shepheardes Calender* when it first appeared in 1579, is thought by some to have been Edward Kirke (a Cambridge contemporary of Spenser's), by others, Spenser himself.

is posed again by the terms of the Red Cross Knight's farewell to Guyon:

> But you, faire Sir, whose pageant next ensewes,
> Well mote yee thee,[1] as well can wish your thought.
>
> (II, i, 33)

Was *The Faerie Queene* originally the 'Pageants' referred to by E. K.? Whether this is so or not, the poem is in any case very often to be regarded as a verbalization of Pageant.

By Pageant is meant a procession or group of symbolical figures in symbolical costume, often in symbolical surroundings. Take, for example, the opening of *The Faerie Queene*, in which Una, the descendant 'of ancient Kings and Queenes', appears leading 'in a line a milke white lambe' (I, i, 4f.). Just such a group occurred in a piece of actual historical pageantry at a feast given by Henry V for the Emperor Sigismund. One of the 'sotiltes' or ornamental devices used in serving the food on that occasion was 'a Castell and saynt George and the kynges doughter ledyng the lambe yn atte the Castell yates'.[2] This comparison helps us to get in its right perspective a feature of the *Faerie Queene* passage that would otherwise seem a blemish: namely, that Una's lamb is forgotten the moment it has been mentioned, and never afterwards brought back into the poem. For, just as a pageant or a masque is not completely dramatic, so Spenser's art is not completely narrative. Instead we are meant to *look* and to see the *shows* it presents.

[1] Thrive.
[2] *The Great Chronicle of London*, ed. A. H. Thomas and I. D. Thornley (1938), 95. The king's daughter and the lamb also appear in the 1461 Bristol pageant mentioned below, p. 90.

More correctly, Pageant is, of course, only one member of a wider class of contemporary forms in which meaning was conveyed iconographically. Throughout this whole system of iconography, Spenser ranged freely, verbalizing now one form, now another. And the material at his disposal was very various. It included:

1. *Pageant Proper*. Actual pageants often presented figures as abstract as any in *The Faerie Queene*, and managed to convey their meaning through the dress, arrangement, and posture of the actors. During his 1432 Entry into London, for example, Henry VI was met at London Bridge by Nature, Grace and Fortune, then at Cornhill by Sapience and the Seven Liberal Arts.[1] Occasionally, pageants seem even to have had something of the splendour and strangeness of the world of romance. Thus Froissart, describing Queen Isabel's 1389 Entry into Paris, tells how among many other fantastic devices she came to a huge castle, constructed of wood, in which was a bed called the Bed of Justice:

In this castle there was a plain, for the castle contained a great space, and this plain was full of trees, and full of hares, conies, and birds, that flew in and out: for when they were abroad, they flew thither again for fear of the people. And out of these trees there issued a white hart, and went to the bed of Justice; and out of the other part of the wood there issued out a lion and an eagle properly, and freshly approached the hart, and the bed of Justice. Then came there out of the trees a twelve young maidens richly apparelled, with chaplets of gold on their heads, holding naked swords in their hands: and they

[1] *The Great Chronicle of London*, ed. Thomas and Thornley, 159–63; *Chronicles of London*, ed. C. L. Kingsford (Oxford, 1905), 100–5.

4

went between the hart, the lion, and the eagle, and there they shewed themselves ready to defend the hart and the bed of Justice.[1]

You can see what Dekker meant when he spoke of 'pageants built on Fairie land'.[2]

2. *Tournament Pageantry*. Accounts of medieval and Renaissance tournaments often seem so poetical that it is difficult to believe one is reading about actual events. Moreover, it is usually impossible to draw any distinct line between imaginative creation and literary allusion on the one hand, and factual expressive gesture on the other. At the Pas d'Armes de la Bergère organized by King René of Anjou at Tarascon in 1449, for example, the lists had a shepherdess beside a tree with two shields hanging from it. One of the shields was white to signify Joy, the other black for Melancholy. The challengers were two squires disguised as shepherds.[3] The pageantry at the Great Westminster Tournament of 1511 was even more high-fantastical. The challengers were Ceure Loyall (Henry VIII), Joyous Panser, Bone Valoyr, and Valliaunt Desyre. These four knights from the land of Noble Heart were conveyed round the tilt on a pageant ensconced within 'a mount which was passyng kunnyngly and Curiously wrougth wyth Rokkis treys and dere,' with before it,

---

[1] *The Chronycle of Syr John Froissart*, tr. Lord Berners, iii, 153; ed. Henley, v (1902), 279; spelling modernized.

[2] *Cit.* Per Palme, 'Ut Architectura Poesis', in *Idea and Form*, Uppsala Studies in the History of Art, n.s. i (Stockholm, 1959), 101. (The best introduction to the pageants is George R. Kernodle, *From Art to Theatre: Form and Convention in the Renaissance* (Chicago, 1944).

[3] 'Deux gentilz escuiers pastoureaux'; see *Œuvres complètes du Roi René*, ed. M. le Comte de Quatrebarbes, 4 vols. (Angers, 1845–6), ii, 52, 57 f.; also G. A. Crapelet, *Le Pas d'Armes de la Bergère* (Paris, 1828).

between two pillars, a virgin in blue and light tawny satin making a garland of rosemary. The whole was drawn by a beaten gold leopard and a beaten silver antelope, led by two woodwoses.[1] This last detail reminds us that the Wild Man, whom we too often think of as the invention of poets such as Spenser, was quite a common figure in tournament pageantry. There were even Wild Women. In a Burgundian challenge of 1469, the *Dame Sauvaige*, organized by Claude de Vauldray at Ghent, the challenger a 'savage' lady complete with wooded mountain and cave.[2]

3. *Masque.* In masque, the verbalization of iconography is carried a stage further. Here the case of Ben Jonson is of particular interest. For he sometimes works into the actual text of his plays and masques quite elaborate iconographical stage directions. In an inset masque in the Fifth Act of *Cynthia's Revels*, Cupid presents four ladies, who have come from the palace of Queen Perfection, with these words:

The first, in citron colour, is *naturall Affection*, which given us to procure our good, is somtime called STORGE ... Her device is a *perpendicular Levell*, upon a *Cube*, or *Square*. The word, SE SUO MODULO. Alluding to that true measure of ones selfe, which as everie one ought to make, so is it most conspicuous in thy divine example.

The second, in greene, is AGLAIA, *delectable and pleasant Conversation* ... Her device within *a Ring of clouds, a Heart with shine about it*. The word, CURARUM NUBILA PELLO. An

[1] *The Great Chronicle of London*, ed. Thomas and Thornley, 368–74.

[2] See Olivier de la Marche, 'Traicté d'un Tournoy tenu à Gant', printed in B. Prost, *Traicté de la forme et devis comme on faict les Tournois* (Paris, 1878), 55–95.

allegorie of CYNTHIAES light, which no lesse cleares the skie,
then her faire mirth the heart.

The third, in the discolour'd mantle spangled all over, is
EUPHANTASTE, *a well conceited Wittinesse* . . . Her device, upon
a *Petasus,* or *Mercuriall* hat, a *Crescent.* The word, SIC LAUS
INGENII. Inferring, that the praise and glorie of wit, doth ever
increase, as doth thy growing moone.

The fourth in white, is APHELEIA, a *Nymph* as pure and
simple as the soule, or as an abrase table, and is therefore called
Simplicitie; without folds, without pleights, without colour,
without counterfeit: and (to speake plainly) *Plainenesse* it
selfe. Her device is no device. The word under her *silver
Shield,* OMNIS ABEST FUCUS. Alluding to thy spotlesse selfe,
who art as farre from impuritie, as from mortalitie.   (v, vii)

The iconography of masques could be extremely sophisticated. In fact, much of the effort in writing them must
have gone into subtle finessing on the well-known iconographical types, into progressively lightening the touch
in pursuit of the ideal of *multum in parvo.*

4. *Traditional Images of Gods.* A large part of the body of
iconographical information available to Spenser concerned images of the gods. Oddly enough, this kind of
iconography can often be obscure to us because our
notions of the gods are too classically correct. In the
earlier period, images of the gods were not usually derived
from ancient works of art but from descriptions in ancient
poetry, worked over in medieval style. Again, the iconography of the gods was a good deal influenced (as Fritz
Saxl showed) by Arabic astrological images. Thus Juno
may have a veil because she symbolizes Memory, and
recollection of sin causes shame; while Mercury may

appear as a scribe because of confusion with the Babylonian god Nebo.[1]

5. *Hieroglyphs and Emblems.* The hieroglyphic tradition stems very largely from one man, Horapollo, an Egyptian Greek (A.D. 408–?450), who wrote a book that professes to give the inner meaning of various hieroglyphic symbols. (The meaning disclosed usually turns out, but only in the end, to be a platitude.) This peculiar work was discovered in the West in 1419, and was published by Aldus in 1505 as the *Hieroglyphica*. It soon became enormously influential, and fathered a vast family of far superior emblem books and symbologies. Its greatest offspring along the former line was Andrea Alciati's *Emblematum liber*;[2] along the latter, Pierio Valeriano's *Hieroglyphica*.[3]

6. *Philosophical Iconography.* Working over this hieroglyphic tradition—and over Plutarch's anthropological syncretism and Plato's philosophical mythology besides—come the Florentine Platonists Marsilio Ficino[4] and

[1] See Jean Seznec, *The Survival of the Pagan Gods*, tr. Barbara F. Sessions, Bollingen Series, xxxviii (New York, 1953), 94, 158f.

[2] Augsburg, 1531. There is a good bibliography of emblem books in Mario Praz, *Studies in Seventeenth-Century Imagery* (Rome, 1964).

[3] Basel, 1556. Other works of this kind include Fortunio Liceti's *Hieroglyphica* (Padua, 1653); Filippo Picinelli's *Mondo simbolico* (Milan, 1653); and Athanasius Kircher's *Oedipus Aegyptiacus*, 3 vols. (Rome, 1652–4).

[4] Marsilio Ficino (1433–99) devoted much of his life to translating and interpreting the principal texts of ancient Platonism. He also developed his own mode (it is hardly a system) of thought, which might be described as rationalized Christian Neoplatonism. In 1462 he became head of the Florentine Platonic Academy; in 1473 he was ordained a priest. Ficino's excellent translations from Plato and Plotinus, and his commentaries on certain of their works, were the main conduit by which Platonic ideas reached Renaissance Europe. Of the commentaries, the most influential, that on the *Symposium*, has been translated into English and edited by Sears R. Jayne as *Marsilio Ficino's Com-*

Giovanni Pico della Mirandola.[1] They believed not only that all myths and hieroglyphics hide a profound meaning but also that this ancient pagan under-meaning is really in agreement with Christianity. The great Italian mythical pictures are deeply influenced by the views of the Florentine Neoplatonists, so that it is hardly an exaggeration to speak of a tradition of philosophical iconography.[2]

Spenser lived in a society that had inherited this whole

mentary on Plato's 'Symposium', Univ. of Missouri Studies, xix (Columbia, Missouri, 1944). The worth of Ficino's philosophy, as distinct from his scholarship, has become debatable; but there can be no question that it now receives less attention than it deserves. On love, on friendship, and on the contemplative life, his thought is deep and worth any man's time. A facsimile reprint of the 1576 Basel edition of Ficino's collected works has been edited by Mario Sancipriano and Paul Oskar Kristeller (Turin, 1959-); and his thought is studied in Kristeller's *The Philosophy of Marsilio Ficino*, tr. Virginia Conant (New York, 1943).

[1] Giovanni Pico della Mirandola (1463–94) was only less important than Ficino as an exponent of Platonic theology, in spite of the fact that he had wider interests and was in a sense less of a specialist. Even by Renaissance standards his education was broad: in addition to law and Aristotelian philosophy, he studied Aramaic, Arabic, and Hebrew, the last of which led him on to the Jewish Cabala. The *Heptaplus* on Genesis, like much of his writing, shows a strong disposition to find truth, or 'vestiges' of truth, in every doctrine whatsoever (except those of the astrologers). This syncretistic tendency running through his thought is studied in Edgar Wind's *Pagan Mysteries in the Renaissance* (1958). It inspired Pico's most ambitious project, a harmony of Plato and Aristotle, of which the completed *De ente et uno* was to form a part. Although at first associated with the Florentine Academy, he was always more extreme and more ascetic than Ficino, and towards the end of his short life he came under the sway of Savonarola. Pico's collected works first appeared as the *Commentationes Joannis Pici Mirandulae*, 2 parts (Bologna, 1495–6), then as *Omnia opera* (Venice, 1498); a modern reprint is being edited by E. Garin (Florence, 1942-). The famous oration *De hominis dignitate* has been translated by Elizabeth L. Forbes (Lexington, 1953) and by A. Robert Caponigri (Chicago, 1956). His cabalism is discussed in J. Blau, *The Christian Interpretation of the Cabala in the Renaissance* (New York, 1944).

[2] A good example of a work in this tradition is Botticelli's *Primavera*, the philosophical meaning of which is illuminatingly discussed by Professor Wind in *Pagan Mysteries in the Renaissance*, ch. 7.

complex of iconographical traditions. By his time the iconographic art had travelled far from mere pageants, and was very much a learned art. In assimilating the tradition, therefore, his first step would be to get the images *right*. For the Renaissance poet this was a *sine qua non*. To begin with, he would use for the purpose such handbooks as Cartari's *Le imagini de i dei* (1556). Professor Seznec has shown the extent to which this book and others like it were designed as practical working manuals. Thus, in his Preface to Cartari's *Le imagini*, Francesco Marcolini hopes that the work 'will be welcome to painters and sculptors',[1] while Tritonio, writing in 1560, claims that in his *Mythologia* he has collected examples out of Ovid 'in such a way that they could be adapted to almost anything in writing a poem'. But Spenser, first a pupil in the iconographic art, later became himself an authority. We find Henry Peacham in his *Graphice* (1612) advising everyone to follow Spenser's images of August and of Fear. And for a century and more both poets and novelists were to treat *The Faerie Queene* as a convenient store of models for emblematic description.

If we want to know whether an artist could work under such iconographical chains, with their innumerable fine links of predetermined detail, we have only to look for our answer to Botticelli. Far from imprisoning, icono-

[1] 'Sarà molto utile anchora a chi si piglia piacere di conoscere le antichità, et è per giovare non poco alli Dipintori, et a gli Scultori, dando loro argomento di mille belle inventioni da potere adornare le loro statoe, e le dipinte tavole. E forse anchora che i Poeti et i dicitori di prose ne trovanno giovamento...'

graphy was for him an inheritance that set him free to be
an artist. His art is original—but only as art. Accepting
traditional images, he loads them with wisdom from the
philosophers and disposes them in divine compositions.
And so, in my opinion, does Spenser.

But, if it was a learned art, iconography was also
essentially a public one. We often talk of the Elizabethan
stage projecting out into the audience and involving them,
so that real life merged into its portrayal in the performance. And with all this iconography it was much the
same. It existed to decorate public buildings, to solemnize
public processions, to inform public occasions with visual
meaning. (One reason why the images had to be correct,
indeed, was so that they could be generally recognized.)
Art as it is known to us can sometimes peep into a world
other than our own; but this was art jutting out into life,
and life turning into art. Thus the knights in a tournament
were at once athletes, engaged in a real (even a dangerous)
game, and characters, from an imaginary story: just as,
in *Comus*, the maskers were both imaginary people in a
wood encountering spirits, and real people in a ban-
queting hall complimenting Lord Bridgewater.

Iconographical art was not a comment on life, so much
as a continual statement of it—an accompaniment, rather
than a criticism. Or, if you wish, life itself, in another
mode. The planets (it said), the Virtues, the Vices, the
Liberal Arts, the Worthies, are *thus*. If now we were to
use a similar art, it would be full of figures symbolizing
the atom, evolution, relativity, totalitarianism, demo-
cracy, and so on.

All this helps to put two things about Spenser in a new light. One is his propensity for mingling the Christian and the pagan. Take for example the simile used to describe the angel who sits by Guyon's head after the ordeal of the cave of Mammon:

> Like as *Cupido* on *Idaean* hill,
>> When having laid his cruell bow away,
>> And mortall arrowes, wherewith he doth fill
>> The world with murdrous spoiles and bloudie pray,
>> With his faire mother he him dights[1] to play,
>> And with his goodly sisters, *Graces* three.

(II, viii, 6)

Now it would be a commonplace, to Spenser's early readers, that by Cupid the ancients meant either human or celestial love.[2] Similarly with Cupid's 'goodly sisters', who have by no means been dragged in just for a bit of mythological embellishment. We are meant to think of them as they appear, say, in the medal of Pico della Mirandola: as Pulchritudo, Amor, and Voluptas. And, as Professor Wind has shown, this triad is derived from Ficino's description of the circle of divine love:

The circle . . . so far as it takes its beginning in God and attracts, is Beauty; so far as it goes forth into the world and moves it to rapture, it is Love, and so far as it returns to its origin and unites with the creator his creation, it is Beatitude. Amor starts from Pulchritudo and ends in Voluptas.[3]

[1] Prepares, goes.
[2] Nicholas of Cusa, writing in 1440, says that the pagans 'took their names for God from the different qualities of creatures'. Among many other names they called him Cupid 'on account of the mutual love of the two sexes'. See *De docta ignorantia*, i, 25; tr. Fr Germain Heron (1954), 57.
[3] *In Platonis Convivium*, ii, 2, *cit*. Wind, *Pagan Mysteries*, 50.

Introduction

Or take the description of the Mount of Contemplation ascended by the Red Cross Knight, which is compared first to the Mount of Olives and then to Parnassus:

> Or like that sacred hill, whose head full hie,
>> Adornd with fruitfull Olives all arownd,
>> Is, as it were for endlesse memory
>> Of that deare Lord, who oft thereon was fownd,
>> For ever with a flowring girlond crownd:
>> Or like that pleasaunt Mount, that is for ay
>> Through famous Poets verse each where renownd,
>> On which the thrise three learned Ladies play
> Their heavenly notes, and make full many a lovely lay.
>
> (I, x, 54)

At first it may seem tasteless to speak of Christ's inspiration and the poet's in the one stanza. But to those who thought in the tradition I have been describing it would not have seemed so. For they regarded poetry, and especially ancient poetry, as a veiled form of theology. Boccaccio put it most extremely (and perhaps not wholly disingenuously) when he wrote in his *Vita di Dante* that 'the ancient poets, so far as it is possible to human capacity, followed in the footsteps of the Holy Spirit ... theology and poetry are in agreement as to their form of working ... not merely is poetry theology but theology is poetry'.[1] But we have no reason to suspect the motives of Pico when he proposed to write a book about poetic theology to explain how the ancients covered divine knowledge 'with enigmatic veils and poetic dissimula-

[1] Ch. 22; tr. A. H. Gilbert in *Literary Criticism: Plato to Dryden* (New York, 1940), 208–11.

tion.'[1] Similarly Gavin Douglas devoted the whole of his Sixth Prologue to showing that

> In all his warkis Virgil doith discrive
> The stait of man, gif thou list understand.
>
> Twichand our faith mony clausis he fand
> Quhilk beyn conform, or than collaterall.[2]

And Sidney concludes his *Defence* with an appeal to his reader to respect the 'sacred misteries' of poetry, and

> to beleeve, with *Clauserus* . . . that it pleased the heavenly deitie by *Hesiod* and *Homer*, under the vaile of Fables to give us all knowledge, *Logicke*, *Rhetoricke*, *Philosophie*, naturall and morall, and *Quid non?* To beleeve with me, that there are many misteries contained in *Poetrie*, which of purpose were written darkly, least by prophane wits it should be abused: To beleeve with *Landin*, that they are so beloved of the Gods, that whatsoever they write, proceeds of a divine furie.[3]

Thus the two inspirations, which at first seemed so disparate and so tastelessly juxtaposed in Spenser's stanza, turn out to have been forms of the same inspiration. Divine Wisdom spoke not only on the Mount of Olives, but also on Parnassus.

Similarly with the description of Nature in the *Cantos of Mutabilitie*:

> Her garment was so bright and wondrous sheene,
> That my fraile wit cannot devize to what
> It to compare, nor finde like stuffe to that,

[1] See Wind, *Pagan Mysteries*, 24.

[2] I.e. 'In all his works Virgil sets forth the state of man, if you care to interpret him . . . As far as the Faith is concerned, he explores many doctrines that are in conformity with it, or (as it were) parallel.' *Virgil's Aeneid*, ed. D. F. C. Coldwell, S. T. S., vol. iii (1959), p. 2.

[3] *The Defence of Poesie* in *The Complete Works of Sir Philip Sidney*, ed. A. Feuillerat, 4 vols. (Cambridge, 1912–26), iii, 45.

Introduction

> As those three sacred *Saints*, though else most wise,
> Yet on mount *Thabor* quite their wits forgat,
> When they their glorious Lord in strange disguise
> Transfigur'd sawe; his garments so did daze their eyes.
>
> (VII, vii, 7)

I think that Spenser's Nature is really an image of God himself. This view is borne out, indeed, by a speech of Mutabilitie's a few stanzas later: 'For, even the gods to thee, as men to gods do seeme' (VII, vii, 15). As for the name *Nature*, it need present no difficulty. As Nicholas of Cusa[1] reminds us, the ancients called God Nature.[2] In an adjacent passage, we find a concept of deity which corresponds more closely still with Spenser's Nature. Cusanus says that in the Divine One all differences coincide:

Who can understand the infinite unity that infinitely transcends and precedes all distinction—which, without being a composite, embraces all in its absolute unity—in which there is neither diversity nor difference and where man does not differ from lion nor heaven from earth?[3]

So Spenser's Nature is veiled, some say, to conceal her terror, 'for that her face did like a Lion shew' (VII, vii, 6).

---

[1] Nicolaus Cusanus (1401–64) takes his name from his birthplace, Cues on the Moselle. He was a reforming churchman before the Reformation; yet in spite of the independence of his thought he achieved the rank of cardinal. As a speculative philosopher of paradox, and a Christian Platonist, he was the most illustrious exponent of a mode of thought that Spenser in his different medium often adapts. The *De docta ignorantia* appeared in 1440. On the basis of this work Cusanus has a claim to be considered the first relativist. See, e.g., his account of the implications of the Earth's movement: 'every man, whether he be on earth, in the sun or on another planet, always has the impression that all other things are in movement whilst he himself is in a sort of immovable centre . . . In consequence, there will be a machina mundi whose centre, so to speak, is everywhere, whose circumference is nowhere' (ii, 12; tr. Heron, 111).

[2] *Ibid.* i, 25; tr. Heron, 57.   [3] *Ibid.* i, 24; tr. Heron, 54.

The Venus of the temple entered by Scudamour is similarly veiled to conceal the coincidence of contraries. With her, however, the coincidence takes the form of hermaphroditism. The reason for her veil is 'hard to know', since her priests keep it an esoteric mystery; but it is said to be because

> she hath both kinds[1] in one,
> Both male and female, both under one name:
> She syre and mother is her selfe alone,
> Begets and eke conceives, ne needeth other none.
>
> (IV, X, 41)

This has an obvious meaning at the level of human sexuality. But Venus, says Cusanus, was also a name for God. The universal means of generation is sexual, so that 'Hermes[2] ... argued, in consequence, that the Cause of All, God, comprised in Himself the masculine and feminine sexes ... Valerius Romanus also shared this view and sang of an omnipotent Jupiter who was God the father and God the mother.'[3] Both Spenser's veiled Venus and his veiled Nature, therefore, are to be regarded as symbols of God. As such, their images are appropriately constructed of elements drawn both from Christian revelation and from the intimations of poetic theology.

The other thing that is put in a new light is the so-called 'historical allegory'. This term is usually taken to mean that the whole of *The Faerie Queene* is a *roman à clef*, which can be understood only when you have found the

---

[1] Sexes, natures.

[2] I.e. Hermes Trismegistus, or 'Thoth the very great,' the reputed author of the large body of occult mystical treatises known as the *Corpus Hermeticum*. These are late antique works, written in Egypt by authors of Greek speech, dealing with astrological, philosophical, or theological topics in a pious but unperspicuous way. [3] *De docta ignorantia*, i, 25; tr. Heron, 57.

historical interpretation. Now passages of that kind can in fact be found. But usually the real process of reading the poem is almost exactly the opposite. Take an example of an obvious historical allegory in a pageant. Queen Elizabeth I in procession comes to a conduit. Here an allegorical welcoming party has been assembled. Mercy, Chastity, and Beauty hail her as their sister, abdicate in her favour, and present her with a crown. Undoubtedly historical allegory. Yet there is no question whatsoever of explaining the abstract figures by reference to the Queen. Indeed, they are self-explanatory. It is the Queen, instead, who is being equated and complimented by momentary identification with them. And so it is with *The Faerie Queene*. We should not say 'To appreciate Belphoebe we must think about Elizabeth I'; but rather 'To understand the ritual compliment Spenser is paying Elizabeth, we must study Belphoebe.' The movement of the interpreting mind is from the real people into the work of art, not out of the work to them. For, after all, the end of the process is supposed to be the recovered work of art. In short, for the reader of *The Faerie Queene* the historical is a point of departure, and no more than that.

We should expect, then, from Spenser's poem, a simple fairy-tale pleasure sophisticated by polyphonic technique, a simple 'moral' sophisticated by a learned iconography. Moreover, we should expect to find all of these reacting on one another, to produce a work very different from what we are used to. And now it is time to catch hold of one thread of the fabric, and pull.

CHAPTER I

THE FALSE CUPID

Blindfold he was, and in his cruell fist
    A mortall bow and arrowes keene did hold,
    With which he shot at randon, when him list,
    Some headed with sad[1] lead, some with pure gold;
    (Ah man beware, how thou those darts behold)
    A wounded Dragon under him did ly,
    Whose hideous tayle his left foot did enfold,
    And with a shaft was shot through either eye,
That no man forth might draw, ne no man remedye.
                                   (III, xi, 48)

This stanza provides examples of nearly everything in
Spenser that tends to disappoint a modern reader. To
begin with, the movement of the verse is extremely
regular: only in the fourth line ('Some headed with sád
leád, some with púre góld') is the iambic flow disturbed.
Then, the image presented appears banal. We have heard
a thousand times before that Cupid is blindfold and that
he bears arrows. Even the distinction between two kinds of
arrows is not new. We have met it in Ovid's *Metamorphoses* (i, 463 ff.) and in the *Roman de la Rose*.[2] Worse

---

[1] Punning between 'causing sorrow' (*OED*, A, I, 5, f) and 'dense, massive,
heavy' (*OED*, A, II, 7, a). In the latter sense cf. Gavin Douglas, *Aeneis*, xi, 47:
'The schaft was sad and sound, and weill ybaik' (well hardened with heat).

[2] Ll. 939 ff.: Cupid's beloved friend Sweet-Looks bears two bows, one evil,
one good:

    Moreover in his hands were seen
    Ten arrows, five of which were fair
    And beauteous, these his right hand bare,
    Brilliant the plumes, the notches made
    Of gold, the while like-precious blade

The False Cupid

still, there are no tensions or ambiguities in the language—nothing but literal, sequacious description. The only novelty is the dragon under Cupid's foot. The only puzzle is the shaft which has put out its eyes, and the curious emphasis (in the last line) on the hopeless character of the injury. It sounds almost as if Spenser were pitying the dragon. And no one expects a writer of chivalrous romance to pity dragons.

Such a passage cannot be said to demand, or even to admit, the minute verbal explication in which the most vigorous modern criticism excels. There is, however, room for explication of a different sort. For, though the conventional attributes may assist recognition of the 'Image all alone' to which they belong (for he has not been named), they are not meant just as identification labels. Cupid's arrows, generally banal, are not banal in Spenser. After all, the mythology of Cupid and Venus is one of the central interests of the poem. Its very frontispiece (I, Proem, 3) finds a place for 'fair Venus sonne' and for the loves of Venus and Mars. In the *Odyssey* those loves were little more than a merry tale; but by Spenser's

> Each shaft-end wore; though nought of steel
> Or iron knew they, hearts would feel
> Their wound-stroke sorely. Save the shaft
> And plumes, 'twas well-skilled goldsmiths' craft
> Had wrought these weapons; they were capped
> With cruel barbs, and whoso happed
> Within their murderous range to fall
> Would feel Love's wound and own his thrall.

These five arrows were Beauty, Simplicity, Courtesy, Companionship, and Fair-Seeming. In his left hand Sweet-Looks held five other arrows: Pride, Villainy, Shame, Despair, and Infidelity. These were

> Far different, formed of iron fell
> And black as he who rules dark hell.

19

2-22-2

time they had come to symbolize generalized relations of values: the victory of beauty over strength and peace over war, perhaps; or concord's resolution of discord. Already this is what the story meant to Lucretius and to Plutarch. And this is what it meant also to Botticelli, in whose picture of *Mars and Venus* the profound sleep of Mars and the waking tranquillity of Venus powerfully present 'the lineaments of gratified desire': not *their* desire only but desire itself, the desire of all creation. The disarmament of Botticelli's Mars is emphasized by the fact that his arms have become toys for infant fauns to play with. But Spenser introduces a different variation of the disarmament image. He disarms Cupid as well as Mars:

> Lay now thy deadly Heben[1] bow apart,
>> And with thy mother milde come to mine ayde:
>> Come both, and with you bring triumphant *Mart*,
>> In loves and gentle jollities arrayd,
> After his murdrous spoiles and bloudy rage allayd.
>
> (I, Proem, 3)

It is a Cupid without his 'deadly Heben bowe' who inspires the *concubitus* whereby the goddess Harmony is engendered.

And this is not the only passage in the poem where Cupid is deprived of his weapons. The angel in II, viii, 6 is compared not simply to Cupid but to Cupid sporting with the Graces and 'having laid his cruell bow away'. Again, Cupid himself is admitted to the House of Alma

> having from him layd
> His cruell bow... (II, ix, 34)

[1] Ebony.

The False Cupid

—just as in the Garden of Adonis he takes his pleasure
laying his sad darts
Aside...   (III, vi, 49)

There are, admittedly, places where the arrows are
mentioned more perfunctorily: I, Proem, 3 itself, for
example, or III, ii, 26, or III, ii, 35, or III, vi, 23. In these
passages the arrows have a merely rhetorical existence.
They colour the language but they barely reach the
imagination.[1] When they are included in a fully realized
image, however, or expressly excluded from it, they
usually have some definite significance. The presence of
the arrows in the stanza we are considering, therefore,
stamps this Cupid as a particular kind of Cupid.

Similarly with the bandage on Cupid's eyes. It would
be banal if we stopped reading when we had finished this
stanza. But presently it is going to leap into meaning.
We shall then see the living Cupid (so far we have been
looking at his statue) equally blindfold—at first. But
later he unbinds the bandage to enjoy the sight of
Amoret's torture, 'Which seene, he much rejoyced in
his cruell mind'. Proud of the pain, he shakes the darts

---

[1] When Britomart saw Arthegall in the magic glass, she was unaware that
she had taken hurt:

But the false Archer, which that arrow shot
So slyly, that she did not feele the wound,
Did smyle full smoothly at her weetlesse wofull stound.

Later Glauce comforts her with the thought that   (III, ii, 26)

That blinded God, which hath ye blindly smit,
Another arrow hath your lovers hart to hit.   (III, ii, 35)

At III, vi, 23 Venus searching for Cupid fears that he may disguise himself as one
of Diana's nymphs

And turne his arrowes to their exercize:
So may he long himselfe full easie hide.

in his right hand 'full dreadfully', and claps his wings.[1]
He is blind except to the pleasures of cruelty; to them,
gladly attentive.

And what of the wounded dragon under the statue of
Cupid? Dragons (or serpents) can have a great variety of
meanings. To modern depth-psychology they can be
symbols of *libido*, or even of the phallus. In some contexts
they have represented wisdom. Sometimes, if they have
their tails in their mouths, they are emblems of eternity.
But the key to the meaning of this particular type of
dragon lies elsewhere. In Alciati's *Emblematum liber* (1531)
we find the virgin goddess Minerva (or Pallas) pictured
with a dragon as her attendant. The verses that follow
explain why:

> Vera haec effigies innuptae Palladis, eius
> Hic Draco, qui dominae constitit ante pedes.

[1] See III, xii, 22–3:

> Next after her the winged God himselfe
> Came riding on a Lion ravenous,
> Taught to obay the menage of that Elfe,
> That man and beast with powre imperious
> Subdeweth to his kingdome tyrannous:
> His blindfold eyes he bad a while unbind,
> That his proud spoyle of that same dolorous
> Faire Dame he might behold in perfect kind;
> Which seene, he much rejoyced in his cruell mind.
>
> Of which full proud, himselfe up rearing hye,
> He looked round about with sterne disdaine;
> And did survay his goodly company:
> And marshalling the evill ordered traine,
> With that the darts which his right hand did straine,
> Full dreadfully he shooke that all did quake,
> And clapt on hie his coulourd winges twaine,
> That all his many[1] it affraide did make:
> Tho[2] blinding him againe, his way he forth did take.
>
> > [1] Company.   [2] Then.

The False Cupid

Cur divae Comes hoc animal? custodia rerum
   Huic data, sic lucos, sacraque templa colit,
Innuptas opus est cura asservare puellas,
   Pervigili, laqueos undique tendit amor.[1]

A long tradition of dragon-guardians lies behind this emblem. The Golden Fleece was guarded by a dragon, and the dragon that preserves buried treasure (as in *Beowulf*, or the Volsung story) is at least as old as the gold-guarding griffin of the Roman fabulist Phaedrus.[2] More relevant than either of these, however, is the dragon of the Hesperides. The Hesperides themselves associate it with virginity, and so—more potently and on a deeper level—do the golden apples. For apples often symbolize the female breasts: especially, perhaps, girlish and undeveloped breasts, the *pome acerbe* ('unripe' apples) of Ariosto's Alcina in the *Furioso* (vii, 14) or those of Philoclea in the *Arcadia* (1590, I, xiii, 6).

Alciati's book was so well known that we may be sure that it is the source, directly or indirectly, of Spenser's blinded dragon. This too is a guardian of chastity, and a guardian mutilated in the very organ that qualified it for guardianship. Would this meaning have been easily accessible to Spenser's first readers? We cannot be sure. But at least the same function is allotted to the dragon, with the same emphasis on its eyes, by two other English poets. Thus in Jonson:

[1] Andrea Alciati, *Emblematum Liber* (Augsburg, 1531), Embl. 43: 'This is the true likeness of unwedded Pallas. Hers is this dragon, standing at its mistress's feet. Why is this animal the goddess's companion? Its allotted task is to guard things. Thus it cares for groves and sacred temples. Sleepless care is needed to keep girls safe before marriage; love spreads his snares everywhere.'

[2] *Fabulae*, iv, 20, 'Vulpis et draco'.

what earthy spirit but will attempt
To taste the fruite of beauties golden tree,
When leaden sleepe seales up the dragons eyes?
                (*Every man in his Humor*, 1601, III, i, 19–21)

And in Milton:

But beauty like the fair Hesperian Tree
Laden with blooming gold, had need the guard
Of dragon watch with uninchanted eye,
To save her blossoms, and defend her fruit
From the rash hand of bold Incontinence.
                (*Comus*, 393–7)

Without passing the bounds of the single stanza, then, we discover that this image of Cupid is more individualized than it seemed at the first glance. But let us now pass these bounds.

In the stanza immediately preceding we read that the Cupid is made of 'massy gold' (III, xi, 47). Gold in itself would never, I believe, be a symbol of evil to any human poet. But in this particular context Spenser has already contrived to make gold sinister. The statue stands in a room whose walls are covered with tapestries in which

the rich metall lurked privily,
As faining to be hid from envious eye;
Yet here, and there, and every where unwares
It shewd it selfe, and shone unwillingly;
Like a discolourd Snake, whose hidden snares
Through the greene gras his long bright burnisht backe declares.
                (III, xi, 28)

Again, if we go forward from the stanza we started with, we discover that the golden image of Cupid is not merely decorative. It is, in the full theological sense, an idol. And its effect on Britomart, through whose eyes we are seeing the whole adventure, is very remarkable. It 'amazed' her; she couldn't stop looking at it; she was 'dazed' (dazzled and confused) by its extreme brightness. Now Britomart, we know, is the knight of Chastity. But Chastity, as she embodies it, means for Spenser True Love, that is, constant, fertile, monogamous, felicific love. Though she is, during the action of the poem, a virgin, if she is considered mythologically she will seem much more like a mother goddess than a virgin goddess. We are never for long allowed to forget that she is to be the ancestress of kings and heroes:

> For from thy wombe a famous Progenie
> Shall spring, out of the auncient *Trojan* blood.
>
> (III, iii, 22)

It is love, so conceived, that comes to defeat the cruel Cupid, but that is momentarily dazzled by his idol.

The conception of such an enmity between Cupid— one kind of Cupid—and True Love is also found in a passage in Sidney's *Arcadia*, where Cupid is banished from (of all places) the marriage bed. And it is worth noting that Sidney explicitly specifies the dart of Cupid. In the epithalamium sung by Dycus we read:

> But thou foule *Cupid* syre to lawlesse lust,
> Be thou farre hence with thy empoyson'd darte,
> Which though of glittring golde, shall heere take rust
> Where simple love, which chastnesse doth imparte,
> Avoydes thy hurtfull arte.
>
> (1593, III; ed. Feuillerat, ii, 64)

The 'arrows' of Cupid in ancient tradition meant, I
believe, no more than the sweet-sharp stings of bodily
desire.[1] But it is clear that they cannot mean this when
Spenser or Sidney banishes them from scenes of what is
certainly to be regarded as True Love. For, if the arrows
had their ancient meaning, their absence could only mean
impotence and frigidity. But in both poets lawful and
unlawful loves alike usually seek fruition, and are not, in
the cant sense, 'platonic'.

So much for the traditional iconography. If we are in a
position to read it, it tells us at the outset that we are
looking at an image of an evil and cruel love, and that
that love has triumphed over the obstacles opposed to it.
From this starting-point we can go into the individual
artist's composition.

First, the lead-up. We reach the image of Cupid by
entering a castle,[2] and then by entering a room full of
tapestries:

> the wals yclothed were
> With goodly arras of great majesty,
> Woven with gold and silke so close and nere,
> That the rich metall lurked privily.   (III, xi, 28)

These tapestries depict 'all Cupid's wars'; they are full
of his triumphs and his spoils, 'cruell battels' (St. 29) and

---

[1] See, however, Propertius, *Eleg.* iii, 12, discussed in Erwin Panofsky,
Studies in Iconology (New York and Evanston, 1962), 96, 104, where the arrows
of Cupid seem to inflict wounds of a deeper kind.—F.

[2] A character may enter such an allegorical place of evil either voluntarily
or involuntarily. If involuntarily, he is simply experiencing the vice; if voluntarily, he is resisting and perhaps conquering it. To enter the House of
Busyrane in possession of one's self, one has first to overcome the flames.
This Amoret did not try to do, Scudamour fails to do, and Britomart succeeds
in doing.—F.

'mournfull Tragedyes' (45). About them the border is of broken weapons, 'and a long bloudy river through them rayled' (46). Everywhere, representations of suffering and of pain.

Then comes the golden image of Cupid. And after it, an even richer room: one that is furnished not with tapestry 'made in painefull loome', but with wrought gold—'with pure gold it all was overlayd' (51). Here the significance of the metamorphoses in the tapestries is further clarified. For we are told that

> A thousand monstrous formes therein were made,
> Such as false love doth oft upon him weare.
>
> (III, xi, 51)

The subject of the gold reliefs is similar to that of the tapestries, except that it is mortal conquerors and captains over whom 'cruell love' triumphs and shows his 'merciless intent'. Next, the complete emptiness of the castle is stressed:

> no footings trace,
> Nor wight appear'd, but wastefull emptinesse,
> And solemne silence . . .   (III, xi, 53)

In this room, as in the one before, an epigraph is prominent, inscribed over the inside of the door by which you enter. It says BE BOLD. In this second room the encouragement is also written everywhere else— except on a further door, an iron wicket, which on the contrary has a caution: BE NOT TOO BOLD. (In this false love, it seems, we are tempted to be bold in going a certain distance, and bold in leaving, i.e. exchanging the love for another; but we are not to be too bold in passing what Marvell called the iron gates of life and entering full intimacy.) Then, at midnight, the wicket opens and out comes the Masque of Cupid. Again, as with the tapestries, there is an elaborate description. And now, instead of a statue of Cupid, here is 'the winged God him-selfe', or at least the show of an actor representing him.

But the interesting, and the most significant, feature of all this description is the effect of interlocking it with the story. For we see all this erotic imagery through Brito-mart's eyes. And her response to it is often surprising. Thus, the image of Cupid is perfectly clear to us; but like the rest of the place it is mysterious to her:

> That wondrous sight faire *Britomart* amazed,
> Ne seeing could her wonder satisfie.   (III, xi, 49)

In the same way, the masque is to us perfectly self-explanatory. To Britomart, however, it is completely meaningless. Imagine her experience: after hours of soli-tude and claustrophobia, a ritual of quiet and ordered cruelty, and with none of the participants taking any notice of her. To be ignored, to be unable to interfere, is what gives the episode its quality of dream-reality. On the next night, when Britomart, instead of waiting for the masque to come out, goes in through the iron door, she finds none of the characters of the masque, only the enchanter and his victim. An obsession is not to be dealt with through the appearances it produces; you have to attack the source.

We may step aside here to notice certain general principles about *The Faerie Queene* and about allegory at large, which have already emerged. First there is the

The False Cupid

paradox that, to the characters participating in an allegory, nothing is allegorical. They live in a world compact of wonders, beauties, and terrors, which are mostly quite unintelligible to them. Secondly and contrarily, our own experience while we read an allegory is double. It is divided between sharing the experiences of the characters in the story and looking at their life from somewhere outside it, seeing all the time meanings that are opaque from within.

An important corollary follows from this: that there is usually no *direct* interaction between Spenser's heroes and the major pageants. The interaction takes place, but only indirectly, in the mind of the interpreting and active reader. Thus, at the House of Pride, St George is present during a procession of the Seven Deadly Sins (I, iv, 18–36). But he is there merely as a spectator: he does nothing to them, nor they to him. They exchange neither words nor blows. We, for our part, know that he is himself in a state of sin, having abandoned Una for Duessa. But he is completely unaware that this has anything to do with what he is seeing. Even when at the end of the following canto he leaves the House of Pride, it is for a reason apparently quite extraneous to his spiritual state. He goes because his dwarf has discovered a well-populated dungeon. They get out by a back door, with difficulty finding a footing over heaps of corpses

> like a great Lay-stall
> Of murdred men...   (I, v, 53)

Now for St George this is a very ordinary adventure: naturally if you discover that your hostess is someone like

Morgan le Fay, you clear out. But for us the incident is more significant. We see Sin (even Satan) ruling a whole way of life. All that can be done, to escape it and to escape its consequences, is to leave that whole way of life. There is no compromise, no middle course.

Or take the later episode, in which St George goes to Despair as a knight goes to an ogre, to avenge a previous victim:

> With firie zeale he burnt in courage bold,
> Him to avenge, before his bloud were cold. (i, ix, 37)

There is no talk of feelings or of spiritual condition; it is a simple matter of physical adventure. But it proves impossible to make contact with Despayre at this level. Instead, St George is lured into argument about his own sin, and soon he is on the verge of suicide himself. The dénouement again shows the uncomprehending, almost irrelevant preoccupation of the main characters. For St George is rescued in quite a different way from what we might expect, by Una reminding him of his job:

> Is this the battell, which thou vauntst to fight
> With that fire-mouthed Dragon, horrible and bright?
> (i, ix, 52)

The same is true with the other knights. In the Cave of Mammon, for example, Guyon is not inwardly tempted at all.[1] Neither is Britomart tempted in the House of Busyrane. Who would be, when the nature of the temptation is laid so bare? What Guyon and Britomart meet with is chiefly horror. They have therefore no direct

[1] A similar point is made by Harry Berger Jr in *The Allegorical Temper*, Yale Studies in English, cxxxvii (New Haven, 1957), 30.

The False Cupid

dealings with the pageant characters on the moral plane. And the converse is also true. In the Cave of Mammon episode, for example, Spenser makes use of an old folk-lore motif, the belief that if you eat or sleep in the underworld you will never get back. Always behind Guyon there is a fiend walking, waiting to tear him in pieces if he sleeps, or touches covetously, or tastes (II, vii, 27). And this fiend, though he longs to, is unable to do anything to Guyon directly. For the pageant characters are sealed off from the heroes of the poem, just as much as the heroes are from them. Note, again, the difference in degree of comprehension between the hero and the reader, in the Mammon episode. To Guyon the descent is just another exploit, coming conveniently at a time when he had travelled far, 'yet no adventure found' (II, vii, 2), whereas to us it is an exposition of the bases of all economic and worldly evil. Guyon's faint on breathing again the 'vitall aire' of the upper world belongs, I take it, to the same class with his other experiences—*as he sees them*. Its significance has been debated unnecessarily, for it is mere story.

In one case, the isolation of the main characters becomes more emphatic. When Calidore sees the great pageant of Colin piping among the naked Graces, suddenly it all vanishes:

> But soone as he appeared to their vew,
>> They vanisht all away out of his sight,
>> And cleane were gone, which way he never knew.[1]

[1] VI, x, 18. Here again Spenser exploits a folk-lore motif. It had been used before him by Chaucer: see *The Wife of Bath's Tale*, III (D) 989–96, where the

31

It is perhaps significant that the separation should be most explicit and decisive in the episode in which the poet's own *persona* figures.

The separation effect was probably arrived at unconsciously. It would be natural for Spenser to let the pageant develop itself without interruption. Not that this is his invariable practice. But it is sufficiently regular to have a general effect. Isolation of the main characters is an essential foundation of the poem's quality. What is more, departures from the practice of isolating the hero are fewer than might at first sight appear, even outside the main pageants. For, where there seems to be indisputably direct interaction between the patron knights and the personifications, the action is not always what the knights think it to be. St George, for example, admittedly fights with Orgoglio. But the fight is lost before it begins: he

> haplesse, and eke hopelesse, all in vaine
> Did to him pace, sad battaile to darrayne,[1]
> Disarmd, disgrast, and inwardly dismayde.
>
> (I, vii, 11)

This faintheartedness has nothing to do with the Giant's size or strength. It is because St George has drunk— it seemed unimportant at the time—of the Fountain of Sloth, a fountain made dull and slow because its nymph had forsaken Diana in the chase. What interaction there is

knight, passing a forest, sees twenty-four ladies dancing:

> But certainly, er he cam fully there,
> Vanysshed was this daunce, he nyste[2] where.

[1] To engage in battle.   [2] Knew not.

between the main and the allegorical characters evidently
has no ordinary causation.[1]

We may now return to the image of Cupid. As we
have seen, it is clearly the image of a bad, cruel Cupid.
But what kind of bad Cupid? Certainly a Cupid who is
the enemy of marriage, like the Cupid of the verses from
Sidney already quoted. And the continuation of that
Arcadia stanza gives some indication of the kind of enemy
he is:

> But thou foule *Cupid* syre to lawlesse lust,
> Be thou farre hence with thy empoyson'd darte,
> Which though of glittring golde, shall heere take rust
> Where simple love, which chastnesse doth imparte,
>> Avoydes thy hurtfull arte
>> Not needing charming skill,
>> Such mindes with sweet affections for to fill.

> (1593, III; ed. Feuillerat, ii, 64)

Sidney, and I think Spenser too, is referring to the whole
tradition of polite adultery, which has been written of as
an *art* ever since Ovid's time. Thus, when Britomart
finally enters the inmost room of Busyrane's castle, it is
to find the enchanter 'figuring straunge characters of his
art' (III, xii, 31).

For this identification we have been well prepared.
We had a first glimpse of the false Cupid's art, indeed, as
early as the House of Malecasta episode. The character
of Malecasta's love is declared from the outset in the 'law'

[1] See further in Angus Fletcher, *Allegory: The Theory of a Symbolic Mode*
(Ithaca, N.Y. 1964), ch. 1 ('The Daemonic Agent') and ch. 4 ('Allegorical
Causation: Magic and Ritual Forms').

that her six knights try to impose on St George. If he has
no lady or love, he must do service to Malecasta. If he has,
he must forgo her, or else prove her fairer than Malecasta
and be rewarded with—Malecasta's love. What St
George is defending, then, in the affray outside the castle,
is constancy in love. He refuses, he says, 'To chaunge my
liefe [beloved], and love another Dame' (III, i, 24).
Inside the castle, we find many features that look forward
to the castle of Busyrane. The extreme riches—'The
royall riches and exceeding cost' (III, i, 32)—prefigure
Busyrane's even greater riches; though Malecasta's
house is populous, 'full of Damsels, and of Squires', where
his will be all empty and silent. Throughout the episode
the artfulness of Malecasta is repeatedly emphasized. She
tempts Britomart, as the Venus of her tapestry tempts
Adonis, with enticing 'sleights' (III, i, 35): 'well that art
she knew'. But her entertainment, with its carefully
planned stages symbolized by Gardante and the rest, all
seems false and superficial. Compared to Britomart, who
really loves, Malecasta's knights 'but shadowes beene'
(III, i, 45). This point is most finely made when Malecasta,
having quite failed to convey her meaning to Britomart
by hints, at last

> told her briefe,
> That but if she did lend her short reliefe,
> And do her comfort, she mote algates[1] dye.
> But the chaste damzell, that had never priefe[2]
> Of such malengine[3] and fine forgerie,
> Did easily beleeve her strong extremitie.

[1] Altogether.   [2] Experience.   [3] Deceit, guile, fraud.

Full easie was for her to have beliefe,
>   Who by self-feeling of her feeble sexe,
>   And by long triall of the inward griefe,
>   Wherewith imperious love her hart did vexe,
>   Could judge what paines do loving harts perplexe.
>   Who meanes no guile, be guiled soonest shall,
>   And to faire semblaunce doth light faith annexe.

(III, i, 53–4)

It is a good touch that Britomart should be deceived by
Malecasta's art: that she should believe in these faked
love-sorrows just because she has had so much experience
of real ones.

Much more recently, and on an earthier level, we have
seen the false art of love in Paridell's seduction of Malbecco's wife Hellenore. Indeed, 'So perfect in that art was
Paridell' (III, x, 5) that Cupid himself smiled secretly to
see him operate. The 'learned lover' (as he is significantly
called) uses on Hellenore a technique not unlike Malecasta's:

>   He sigh'd, he sobd, he swownd, he perdy[1] dyde,
>   And cast himselfe on ground her fast besyde:
>   Tho[2] when againe he him bethought to live,
>   He wept, and wayld, and false laments belyde,
>   Saying, but if she Mercie would him give
>   That he mote algates dye, yet did his death forgive.

(III, x, 7)

He can simulate feelings with consummate virtuosity,
never for a moment relinquishing the control of his
purposeful craft.

[1] Truly.   [2] Then.

CHAPTER II

ANTITYPES TO THE FALSE CUPID

Opposed to the image of the false Cupid are several antitypes, images that embody different aspects of love in its true form. One of the most striking of these is in the old ending to Book III, in the 1590 edition of the first three books. The ending was altered, apparently owing to the exigencies of the plot, when Books IV–VI were added in 1596. (Spenser seems to have wanted to keep the complications of Amoret's story unresolved.) But no doubt in the complete *Faerie Queene* the original passage would have been used somewhere else. The discarded stanzas are these:

> At last she came unto the place, where late
> She left *Sir Scudamour* in great distresse,
> Twixt dolour and despight halfe desperate,
> Of his loves succour, of his owne redresse,
> And of the hardie *Britomarts* successe:
> There on the cold earth him now thrown she found,
> In wilfull anguish, and dead heavinesse,
> And to him cald; whose voices knowen sound
> Soon as he heard, himself he reared light from ground.
>
> There did he see, that most on earth him joyd,
> His dearest love, the comfort of his dayes,
> Whose too long absence him had sore annoyd
> And wearied his life with dull delayes:
> Straight he upstarted from the loathed layes,
> And to her ran with hasty egernesse,

36

Antitypes to the False Cupid

Like as a Deare, that greedily embayes[1]
In the coole soile, after long thirstinesse,
Which he in chace endured hath, now nigh breathlesse.

Lightly he clipt[2] her twixt his armes twaine,
  And streightly did embrace her body bright,
  Her body, late the prison of sad paine,
  Now the sweet lodge of love and deare delight:
  But she faire Lady overcommen quight
  Of huge affection, did in pleasure melt,
  And in sweete ravishment pourd out her spright:
  No word they spake, nor earthly thing they felt,
But like two senceles stocks[3] in long embracement dwelt.

Had ye them seene, ye would have surely thought,
  That they had beene that faire *Hermaphrodite*,
  Which that rich *Romane* of white marble wrought,
  And in his costly Bath causd to bee site:
  So seemd those two, as growne together quite,
  That *Britomart* halfe envying their blesse,[4]
  Was much empassiond in her gentle sprite,
  And to her selfe oft wisht like happinesse,
In vaine she wisht, that fate n'ould let her yet possesse.[5]

Thus doe those lovers with sweet countervayle,[6]
  Each other of loves bitter fruit despoile.
  But now my teme begins to faint and fayle,
  All woxen weary of their journall[7] toyle:
  Therefore I will their sweatie yokes assoyle[8]
  At this same furrowes end, till a new day:
  And ye faire Swayns, after your long turmoyle,
  Now cease your worke, and at your pleasure play;
Now cease your worke; to morrow is an holy day.

(1590, III, xii, 43–7)

---

[1] Wallows; moistens himself.   [2] Embraced.
[3] Logs, blocks; lifeless things devoid of sensation.   [4] Bliss.
[5] What fate would not let her yet possess.   [6] Compensation.
[7] Daily.   [8] Unloose.

This passage can be read in a variety of ways. From one point of view it is a simple love scene; that would be the interpretation of the reader of Hazlitt's *Faerie Queene*. But if you decided to read Spenser in that way as a general rule, you would soon start complaining of 'faceless knights'. And even in the present passage you might possibly find the hermaphrodite image in Stanza 46 somewhat repellent. From another point of view, the passage is a metaphoric exposition of true marriage. Read in this way, 'So seemd those two, as growne together quite' becomes a moral and psychological statement: an exact antithesis to the description of Paridell and Hellenore as

> a wanton paire
> Of lovers loosely knit...[1]

It is meant to recall the institution of marriage in Gen. ii. 24: 'they shall be one flesh.' Of true marriage in this Biblical sense, of *henosis*, Spenser's image is obviously a visual emblem. But the image has also a more mysterious content, as we shall see when we come to our next antitype. To understand it more fully, we have to adopt an approach like that of Origen's to the verse from Genesis just quoted: 'Let us learn through the allegory how man is made male and female in the image of God.'[2] Notice: it is the married couple, united in the relation called one flesh, that is the *imago Dei*.

Another antitype to the false Cupid is the image in the

[1] These verses, it should be remarked, do not refer primarily to Paridell and Hellenore embracing; they occur at III, x, 16, during the lovers' flight from the house of Malbecco.

[2] *In Gen. homil.* i, 15; ed. Migne, xii, 158.

Temple of Venus in Book IV. In this case, the contrast
extends to the setting of the image: the Temple is also an
antitype to the whole House of Busyrane. As we saw, one
of the noticeable things about Busyrane's house is its
desertion. You go through room after empty room, all in
silence, and the whole place ignores you: nothing ever
happens until midnight. By contrast, entry into the
Temple is an ordered progression through a whole series
of tests. In other words, it is an *initiation*. Far from being
ignored, Scudamour has to defeat twenty knights before
he even reaches the bridge to the island where the
Temple is placed. At the outer gate of the bridge he has to
pass the porter Doubt, and Delay hiding behind the gate;
at the inner (the Gate of Good Desert) he has to defeat the
hideous Giant Daunger.

Yet if Scudamour's progression to the Temple is
orderly, it leaves no impression of excessive formality.
On the island, he finds an ideal combination of Nature
and Art; it seems

> The onely pleasant and delightfull place,
> That ever troden was of footings trace.
> For all that nature by her mother wit
> Could frame in earth, and forme of substance base,
> Was there, and all that nature did omit,
> Art playing second natures part, supplyed it.

> No tree, that is of count,[1] in greenewood growes,[2]
> From lowest Juniper to Ceder tall,
> No flowre in field, that daintie odour throwes,
> And deckes his branch with blossomes over all,
> But there was planted, or grew naturall:

[1] Account, importance.   [2] Growths.

39

> Nor sense of man so coy[1] and curious nice,[2]
> But there mote find to please it selfe withall;
> Nor hart could wish for any queint device,
> But there it present was, and did fraile sense entice.
>
> (IV, x, 21–2)

Instead of the solemn silence of empty rooms, there is the pleasant sound of water:

> the river rolling still
> With murmure soft, that seem'd to serve the workmans will.
>
> (IV, x, 15)

And where Busyrane had tapestry figures of love, here there are live, happy lovers—thousands of them.

Immediately outside the Temple, Scudamour goes through yet another stage of initiation. He has to pass Concord, an amiable dame who sits in the porch to the Temple, reconciling the half-brothers Love and Hate, who stand on either side of her, 'both strongly armed, as fearing one another' (St. 32). Love and Hate are 'of contrarie natures' and join hands only unwillingly. Nevertheless, Concord can force them to make peace. She is

> Mother of blessed *Peace*, and *Friendship* trew;
> They both her twins, both borne of heavenly seed,
> And she her selfe likewise divinely grew;
> The which right well her workes divine did shew.
>
> (IV, x, 34)

Thus, besides presenting another psychological stage in Scudamour's initiation, the porch of Concord contains a minor image of Cusanus' *natura unialis*.

---

[1] Not ready in response; disdainful.   [2] Particular.

Finally, we come to the image of the 'goddesse selfe'. It stands on an altar of some substance more rare than gold, more rare than the 'precious stone' that Cupid's altar was made of. The substance is bright, and 'brickle' like glass—symbolic, perhaps, of beauty.[1] As with the image of Cupid, there is a serpent. But whereas only Cupid's left foot was enfolded by the dragon, Venus allows the serpent a larger part:

> both her feete and legs together twyned
> Were with a snake, whose head and tail were fast combyned.
> (IV, x, 40)

As we have seen, a serpent in itself can symbolize wisdom; and this may not be irrelevant here. But the more specific form of a serpent with its extremities 'combined' means Eternity.[2]

The front of the image of Venus is 'covered with a slender veile', a feature that provokes a stanza of specula-

[1] IV, x, 39. It seems better to relate the glassy material (which is 'uneath to understand' and neither 'durefull' nor yet 'mouldring clay') to that of the 'glassie globe' made by Merlin, in which Britomart saw a vision of Arthegall (III, ii, 21). It was in turn compared to the magic tower of glass Ptolemy built for Phao—impregnable, 'Yet when his love was false, he with a peaze it brake' (III, ii, 20). In each case the glass symbolizes the conditional durability and completeness of the marriage bond; see Panofsky, *Studies in Iconology*, 162, also my *Spenser and the Numbers of Time* (1964), 124n. In other words, the sexual love of the Temple of Venus is based upon a faithful personal relation.—F.

[2] This is *often* the case, and it may be so here. But Spenser must surely also have meant some allusion to the combined serpent of Janus in Macrobius, *Saturnalia*, I, ix, 12 f., which symbolizes the annual cycle of generation: 'a serpent brought together into a circle, devouring its own tail; so as to show that the world sustains itself out of its own self, and returns upon itself again.' The twining, a distinct motif, signifies either Concord or Necessity; see my *Spenser and the Numbers of Time*, 164 and 157–66 *passim*. Opposite the present passage Lewis has noted a quotation to be worked into a later draft: 'An eternal Power which has purchased on us this the most brickle of things?'—F.

tion. The best explanation arrived at is that it was because, 'they say,' Venus is a Hermaphrodite:

> she hath both kinds in one,
> Both male and female, both under one name:
> She syre and mother is her selfe alone,
> Begets and eke conceives, ne needeth other none.

(IV, X, 41)

This at once ranks the Venus with Scudamour-Amoret in their embrace, and Nature in the *Cantos of Mutabilitie* (VII, vii, 5 f.). All three are images of the *natura unialis*, the ultimate unity that underlies all being. Cusanus, who held that 'infinite unity precedes all distinction...where man does not differ from lion' and (following Hermes) that 'the cause of all comprises in Himself masculine and feminine',[1] would have understood and approved Spenser's meaning. So would Pico, with his doctrine that *contradictoria coincidunt in natura uniali*;[2] or Leone Ebreo, who wrote that 'in God the lover, the beloved, and their love are all one and the same, and although we count them to be three and say that the lover is informed by the beloved and that love derives from them both (as from the father and mother), yet the whole is one simple unity and essence...'[3] But here I must enter a caveat. I am not saying that, for Spenser and Cusanus and the rest, God is Nature is Venus. Nature and Venus (and, for that

[1] *De docta ignorantia*, i, 24 and 25; tr. Heron, 54 and 57. Cf. also the opening of the latter chapter, where Cusanus tells us that the pagans gave God many names, including Venus and Nature.

[2] 'Contradictions are reconciled in the nature of the One', *Conclusiones paradoxae*, no. 15, *Opera omnia* (Basel, 1573), 90.

[3] *The Philosophy of Love (Dialoghi d'Amore)*, tr. F. Friedeberg-Seeley and Jean H. Barnes (1937), 299.

Antitypes to the False Cupid

matter, Scudamour-Amoret) are only expositions, images, or beams of the *natura unialis*.

It remains to ask why the image should be veiled, even if the Venus is hermaphroditic. This is a question that Venus' priests would not answer: indeed, they 'laboured to conceal' the answer (IV, x, 41). And this very fact gives us our clue. For, in the Neoplatonic thought with which I have been connecting the passage, it was fundamental that all great truths should be veiled:

the wise . . . know that a naked and open exposition of herself is distasteful to Nature, who, just as she has withheld an understanding of herself from the vulgar notions of men . . . has also wished her secrets to be treated mythically (*per fabulosa*) by the prudent.[1]

Scudamour prays to Venus in a manner quite in accord with her symbolism of the ultimate unity:

So all the world by thee at first was made,
    And dayly yet thou doest the same repayre.   (IV, x, 47)

Two aspects of Venus are touched on here. In the second line, clearly, she is the planetary deity who by influencing men and beasts to amorousness replenishes the world. The first, however, expresses a less obvious and more audacious idea. To understand it we must turn to *Timaeus* 29, where Plato argues from the beauty of the cosmos that it was made from a pattern no less than eternal.[2] Spenser himself develops the doctrine of a *Paradigma* of creation in

[1] Macrobius, *In somnium Scipionis*, I, ii, 17. A side-note here indicates that in a later draft Lewis would have developed the point that Cupid is absent from the Temple: *amorini* play about the image of Venus 'The whilest their elder brother was away' (IV, x, 42).—F.

[2] 'Now if so be that this Cosmos is beautiful and its Constructor good, it is plain that he fixed his gaze on the Eternal; but if otherwise (which is an impious

43

An Hymne in Honour of Beautie. In good Neoplatonic
fashion he attributes the beauty of the pattern to Venus:

> What time this worlds great workmaister did cast
> To make al things, such as we now behold,
> It seemes that he before his eyes had plast
> A goodly Paterne, to whose perfect mould
> He fashiond them as comely as he could;
> That now so faire and seemely they appeare,
> As nought may be amended any wheare.
>
> That wondrous Paterne wheresoere it bee,
> Whether in earth layd up in secret store,
> Or else in heaven, that no man may it see
> With sinfull eyes, for feare it to deflore,
> Is perfect Beautie which all men adore,
> Whose face and feature doth so much excell
> All mortal sense, that none the same may tell.
>
> . . . .
>
> For through infusion of celestiall powre,
> The duller earth it quickneth with delight,
> And life-full spirits privily doth powre
> Through all the parts, that to the lookers sight
> They seeme to please. That is thy soveraine might,
> O *Cyprian* Queene, which flowing from the beame
> Of thy bright starre, thou into them doest streame.

(ll. 29–42, 50–6)

But there are also implicit in Scudamour's prayer certain other ideas about Venus, which must be deferred
until we come to discuss the Garden of Adonis.

supposition), his gaze was on that which has come into existence. But it is clear
to everyone that his gaze was on the Eternal; for the Cosmos is the fairest of all
that has come into existence, and He the best of all the causes. So having in this
wise come into existence, it has been constructed after the pattern of that which
is apprehensible by reason and thought and is self-identical. Again, if these
premises be granted, it is wholly necessary that this Cosmos should be a Copy
of something' (*Timaeus* 29 A–B; tr. R. G. Bury (1952), 51–3).

CHAPTER III

BELPHOEBE, AMORET, AND THE GARDEN OF ADONIS

I

The two pageants we have mostly been considering, that of the House of Busyrane and that of the Temple of Venus, are directly opposed as bad and good forms of the same thing. Each represents human adult civilized love; though one shows love arduously passing its tests and winning its prize, the other, love trapped, stifled, and turned into a diabolical ritual. What is common to both the House of Busyrane and the Temple of Venus is that they are products of Art. The first is entirely Art, and the second Nature and Art in happy symbiosis. But both show love as a conventional social form.

Now two other pageants have subjects opposite or complementary to these: namely, the Bower of Bliss and the Garden of Adonis. Both Bower and Garden descend to a substratum, and show love not as a social form but as a natural appetite. They also agree in being (or, at least, in purporting to be) products of Nature. But here there is a difference between them, a difference so great that they are themselves opposed, as fundamentally as the House of Busyrane and the Temple of Venus were. For, whereas the Garden is purely and simply natural, the Bower presents a spurious nature, in which the truly natural is excessively enhanced, or even displaced, by the artificial. It is

A place pickt out by choice of best alive,
That natures worke by art can imitate.

(ii, xii, 42)

One would have thought, (so cunningly, the rude,
And scorned parts were mingled with the fine,)
That nature had for wantonesse ensude[1]
Art, and that Art at nature did repine;
So striving each th'other to undermine.

(ii, xii, 59)

Not of course that there is anything wrong with Art in itself. But the Bower is not Art putting itself forward as Art; it is Art trying to deceive, Art substituted for Nature. Even the fruit is not all real fruit: some is of metal, 'So made by art, to beautifie the rest' (St. 55). And yet, 'The art, which all that wrought, appeared in no place' (St. 58): the Bower is an elaborate *trompe l'œil*.

There are also secondary oppositions between the Bower and other images of good forms of love. For example, because the Bower is simply a place of sensuality, it is never shown in act. It presents no action, but only the sensual attractions that lead to action. Thus, Verdant and Acrasia are never actually shown embracing, even if embraces may be supposed to have taken place between them outside the poem. How different with Scudamour and Amoret, whom we see in a variety of adventures, performing a whole range of actions. Their love, when it is held in tableau, in the hermaphroditic image already discussed, is represented by an arrested action. We are shown the moment itself of a physical embrace, though one that is also an ecstasy:

[1] Imitated.

46

> she faire Lady overcommen quight
> Of huge affection, did in pleasure melt,
> And in sweete ravishment pourd out her spright:
> No word they spake, nor earthly thing they felt,
> But like two senceles stocks in long embracement dwelt.
>
> (1590, III, xii, 45)

True love appears as pure action, devoid of sensation.

2

To understand the Garden of Adonis, you have to take it along with the whole myth of Belphoebe and Amoret.

Not the historical allegory of Belphoebe. Certainly Belphoebe 'is' Queen Elizabeth. But we remember the principle established earlier for the interpretation of historical allegory: the meaning of Belphoebe cannot be discovered by thinking about Elizabeth, since Spenser was complimenting Elizabeth by saying that she was like Belphoebe. Indeed, far from having a topical significance, Belphoebe is an archetype. She is a type of the chaste and somewhat terrible Huntress. Behind her lies Artemis, the dread Artemis of the *Hippolytus*. And she will have a new avatar in the Diana of Milton's *Comus*, who embodies, as it happens, a very similar moral ideal:

> 'Tis chastity, my brother, chastity:
> She that has that, is clad in compleat steel,
> And like a quiver'd Nymph with Arrows keen
> May trace huge Forests...
>
> Hence had the huntress *Dian* her dred bow.
>
> gods and men
> Fear'd her stern frown, and she was queen oth' Woods.
>
> (ll. 420–3, 441, 445–6)

47

Belphoebe may seem to contrast in every way with Amoret the melting bride of Scudamour. Yet *contraria coincidunt in natura uniali*, so that the two both turn out to be explications or expositions of the divine beauty and goodness.

This idea is stated twice. The first statement comes in the account of the origin of Amoret and Belphoebe. For we are told that they are jointly the offspring of an immaculate conception, that they were begotten without earthly father. Their mother was Chrysogonee (Gold-birth), the daughter of Amphisa (Both Equal or Equally Both), but their father was Sol himself. Several stanzas are given to the 'goodly storie' of how Amoret and Belphoebe were conceived by Chrysogonee,

> enwombed in the sacred throne
> Of her chaste body...   (III, vi, 5)

by solar beams. Here Spenser introduces a digression, which supports his myth by appealing to the known role of the sun in the physical generation of life. This role is most obvious in the case of 'spontaneous' generation of life in alluvial mud; it is also, however, quite a general one:

> Great father he of generation
> Is rightly cald, th'author of life and light. (III, vi, 9)

The sun is always the ultimate generative power in nature: *hominem generat homo et sol.*[1]

---

[1] Aristotle, *Met.* 1071ᵃ. The tag was still well enough known for Cowley to finesse on it in 'The Parting', *Poems*, ed. A. R. Waller (Cambridge, 1905), 118:

> Thou, who in many a Propriety,
> So truly art the *Sun* to Me,
> Adde one more *likeness*, which I'm sure you can,
> And let *Me* and *my Sun* beget a *Man*.—F.

Belphoebe, Amoret, and the Garden of Adonis

The second statement is reached through a myth of Venus and Diana. Medieval tradition had represented Venus and Diana as perpetually at variance, always in debate or at war. We find them reconciled, however, in the fostering of Belphoebe and Amoret. This reconciliation is presented as a new development, which comes about because Venus has lost Cupid and is searching for him. Now we have noticed before that Cupid can be bad in Spenser. Perhaps, therefore, Spenser's meaning is that the bad Cupid must be removed before the values embodied in Venus and Diana can be reconciled. This theory gains support from the explanation given for Cupid's absence from Venus:

> So from her often he had fled away,
> When she for ought him sharpely did reprove.
>
> (III, vi, 11)

In her search for Cupid, we are told, Venus

> left her heavenly hous,
> The house of goodly formes and faire aspects,
> Whence all the world derives the glorious
> Features of beautie, and all shapes select,
> With which high God his workmanship hath deckt
>
> (III, vi, 12)

—a formulation that almost seems to fuse Venus-as-Paradigma with Venus-as-planetary-deity. After looking in vain in court, city, and country, Venus turns to the forest, and there comes upon Diana. But the Diana she meets is specifically a disarmed and naked Diana, 'asham'd to be so loose surprized' (St. 19). During the quarrel that soon follows, it is Diana who tends to be unpleasant and aggressive, Venus who 'with sugred words and gentle blandishment' pacifies and appeases. Naturally, Venus is after all the deity of peace and reconciliation: that is what all the pictures of Venus subjugating Mars are about.

When Venus and Diana are reconciled, they find Chrysogonee with her two babies. In other words, the qualities represented by Amoret and Belphoebe jointly depend upon a reconciliation of Venus and Diana. Nevertheless, the twins are next distributed between the goddesses for their nurture. Diana takes Belphoebe off to the woods to bring her up as a nymph 'in perfect Maydenhed', while Venus takes Amoret 'in her litle loves stead' (St. 28), and places her in a garden called the Garden of Adonis.

3

But what exactly is this Garden of Adonis? The first thing we are told about it is that Venus brought Amoret

> to her joyous Paradize,
> Where most she wonnes,[1] when she on earth does dwel.
> (III, vi, 29)

It seems fair to conclude that, though it is called the Garden of Adonis, it is really the Garden of Venus. Only of Venus-on-Earth, however: Venus 'when she on earth does dwel'. This tallies with an earlier stanza (12), which has it that when Venus lost Cupid 'Him for to seeke, she left her heavenly hous'.

Now from Ficino's *In Platonis Convivium* we learn that

[1] Lives.

for the Neoplatonic philosopher there are two Veneres,
not one. The first of these 'twin Veneres' is the *Venus
coelestis*, born of Coelus alone, without a mother—
since *mater* interpreted philosophically implies *materia*,
and she is altogether immaterial. She is the Intelligence
in the angelic mind; her region is the region of the cosmic
Mens; and her beauty is the divine splendour that awakens
amor divinus or *caritas* in the human mind. The second
Venus, *Venus vulgaris* or *Venus naturalis*, is born of
Jupiter and Dione. Hers is the power by which things
below are generated (*potentiam, quae inferiora haec generat*);
her region is the region of the *Anima mundi*; and her beauty
is an image of the intelligible beauty, rendered in the
forms she gives to nature and makes available to our
senses.[1] Clearly Spenser's Venus-on-earth resembles more
closely the lower of these two Veneres, the Venus that
Ficino identifies with the *Anima mundi et omnes animae*
(that is, the vital principle in all animals and men—not in
angels, who have no *animae*, but only *mentes* or intellects).
Her function is to procreate; so that the appropriate
abstract term for her might be Fertility or the Life-Force.
When sparkles of the Divine Beauty are poured into the
materiam mundi, they are poured by her.[2]

Thus the Garden of Adonis represents neither a virtue
nor a vice nor any state of mind, but a cosmic operation.
Yet it is one that concerns us all directly: from that garden

[1] *In Platonis Convivium*, ii, 7, 'De duobus amoris generibus, ac de duplici
Venere', in Ficino, *Opera* (Basel, 1576), 1326 f. See Panofsky, *Studies in Iconology*,
142 f.

[2] 'Haec fulgoris illius scintillas in materiam mundi transfundit. Scintillarum
huiusmodi praesentia singula mundi corpora, pro captu naturae, speciosa
videntur.'

we have all come. To it, moreover, we have all returned. For in our own erotic experience we participate in that cosmic operation, just as Spenser did himself:

> well I wote[1] by tryall, that this same
> All other pleasant places doth excell. (III, vi, 29)

The operation is first described almost literally (Sts. 37 f.). The *materia mundi*, continually 'informed'—animated and shaped—and 'reinformed', supplies a vast succession of living creatures. (If it were uninformed altogether, it would lie in Chaos, 'In hatefull darkenesse and in deepe horrore' (St. 36).) Then in a second statement the operation is presented allegorically through the love of Venus and Adonis. Adonis clearly personifies the eternally reformable matter of St. 37. Just as

> That substance is eterne, and bideth so,
> Ne when the life decayes, and forme does fade,
> Doth it consume, and into nothing go,
> But chaunged is, and often altred to and fro

so Adonis

> All[2] be he subject to mortalitie,
> Yet is eterne in mutabilitie,
> And by succession made perpetuall,
> Transformed oft, and chaunged diverslie.
>
> (III, vi, 47)

As for Venus, we are told that in the Garden she 'enjoys Adonis'; and

> when ever that she will,
> Possesseth him ... (III, vi, 46)

The form-giver, in other words, is wedded to matter: *materia appetit formam*. It is, of course, unusual in mytho-

---

[1] Know.   [2] Though.

logy to have the female parent giving form while the
male parent gives matter. And this inversion is emphasized by the application of the passive terms of love to
Adonis, the active—*enjoy, reap, possess, take*—to Venus.
But this is compensated for by the fact that Spenser's
Venus is a goddess, whereas his Adonis is not a god. Nor,
as we shall see, is the inversion without parallels elsewhere
in *The Faerie Queene.*[1]

In between these two portrayals of the cosmic activity
of generation there comes the lament for mutability in
Sts. 39–45:

39

Great enimy to it, and to all the rest,
    That in the *Gardin* of *Adonis* springs,
    Is wicked *Time*, who with his scyth addrest,
    Does mow the flowring herbes and goodly things,
    And all their glory to the ground downe flings,
    Where they doe wither, and are fowly mard:
    He flyes about, and with his flaggy wings
    Beates downe both leaves and buds without regard,
Ne ever pittie may relent his malice hard.

[1] The points made in the present paragraph receive further amplification in
Lewis's review of Robert Ellrodt's *Neoplatonism in the Poetry of Spenser*, in
Études Anglaises, xiv (1961), 107–16, esp. 111 f. A side-note here, which reads
'Son, Bridegroom, King, Shepherd, Priest, Judge', is explained by a passage
in the review: 'on the level of the imagination the masculinity of the Word is
almost impregnably entrenched by the six-fold character of Son, Bridegroom, King, Priest, Judge, and Shepherd. Yet all these, apparently, Spenser
was prepared to break through [in the Sapience of the Fourth Hymn]. After
that, the transference of the sexes between Form and Matter sinks into insig-
nificance.'—F.

40

Yet pittie often did the gods relent,
    To see so faire things mard, and spoyled quight:
    And their great mother *Venus* did lament
    The losse of her deare brood, her deare delight:
    Her hart was pierst with pittie at the sight,
    When walking through the Gardin, them she spyde,
    Yet no'te[1] she find redresse for such despight.
    For all that lives, is subject to that law:
All things decay in time, and to their end do draw.

41

But were it not, that *Time* their troubler is,
    All that in this delightfull Gardin growes,
    Should happie be, and have immortall blis,
    For here all plentie, and all pleasure flowes,
    And sweet love gentle fits emongst them throwes,
    Without fell rancor, or fond gealosie;
    Franckly each paramour his leman knowes,
    Each bird his mate, ne any does envie
Their goodly meriment, and gay felicitie.

42

There is continuall spring, and harvest there
    Continuall, both meeting at one time:
    For both the boughes doe laughing blossomes beare,
    And with fresh colours decke the wanton Prime,
    And eke attonce[2] the heavy trees they clime,
    Which seeme to labour under their fruits lode:
    The whiles the joyous birdes make their pastime
    Emongst the shadie leaves, their sweet abode,
And their true loves without suspition tell abrode.

[1] Might not.   [2] Together.

54

43

Right in the middest of that Paradise,
    There stood a stately Mount, on whose round top
    A gloomy grove of mirtle trees did rise,
    Whose shadie boughes sharpe steele did never lop,
    Nor wicked beasts their tender buds did crop,
    But like a girlond compassed the hight,
    And from their fruitfull sides sweet gum did drop,
    That all the ground with precious deaw bedight,
Threw forth most dainty odours, and most sweet delight.

44

And in the thickest covert of that shade,
    There was a pleasant arbour, not by art,
    But of the trees owne inclination made,
    Which knitting their rancke braunches part to part,
    With wanton yvie twyne entrayld athwart,
    And Eglantine, and Caprifole emong,
    Fashiond above within their inmost part,
    That nether *Phoebus* beams could through them throng,
Nor *Aeolus* sharp blast could worke them any wrong.

45

And all about grew every sort of flowre,
    To which sad lovers were transformd of yore;
    Fresh *Hyacinthus*, *Phoebus* paramoure,
    And dearest love,
    Foolish *Narcisse*, that likes the watry shore,
    Sad *Amaranthus*, made a flowre but late,
    Sad *Amaranthus*, in whose purple gore
    Me seemes I see *Amintas* wretched fate,
To whom sweet Poets verse hath given endlesse date.

Were it not for that, were it not for 'wicked *Time*...
with his scyth addrest', the Garden would be perfect
bliss (St. 41). This lends force and pathos to Spenser's
affirmation that Adonis, though subject to mortality,

may not
For ever die, and ever buried bee.   (III, vi, 47)

For, while we ourselves can do nothing about mortality,
Venus can. Her union with matter—the fertility of nature
—is a continual conquest of death. That is why Matter,
wedded to the *Anima mundi*, may be said to have 'eternall
blis' (St. 48), and why the boar of Chaos is imprisoned
safely in a cave beneath the Garden. Notice, however,
that the boar is not eliminated altogether: we are left
to speculate whether there may at last come a day when
the boar gets out, a day when Nature's self will indeed
vanish.

4

We may now return to Sts. 31–3, where Spenser treats
the gates of the Garden and their keeper Genius:

> It sited was in fruitfull soyle of old,
>> And girt in with two walles on either side;
>> The one of yron, the other of bright gold,
>> That none might thorough breake, nor overstride:
>> And double gates it had, which opened wide,
>> By which both in and out men moten pas;
>> Th'one faire and fresh, the other old and dride:
>> Old *Genius* the porter of them was,
> Old *Genius*, the which a double nature has.

56

He letteth in, he letteth out to wend,
　　All that to come into the world desire;
　　A thousand thousand naked babes attend
　　About him day and night, which doe require,
　　That he with fleshly weedes would them attire:
　　Such as him list, such as eternall fate
　　Ordained hath, he clothes with sinfull mire,
　　And sendeth forth to live in mortall state,
Till they againe returne backe by the hinder gate.

After that they againe returned beene,
　　They in that Gardin planted be againe;
　　And grow afresh, as they had never seene
　　Fleshly corruption, nor mortall paine.
　　Some thousand yeares so doen they there remaine;
　　And then of him are clad with other hew,
　　Or sent into the chaungefull world againe,
　　Till thither they returne, where first they grew:
So like a wheele around they runne from old to new.

In some respects this is the most problematical passage
in the whole canto. The Genius meant is the one who was
anciently a god of fertility and Venus' servant—the
Genius of the *Roman de la Rose* or the *Confessio amantis*.[1]
And the first part of St. 32 is plain enough. We all come
from the Garden, so that we were all once potential beings
waiting for Genius to let us out 'into the world' by the
gate of birth, doubtless the fresh gate in the golden wall
of St. 31. But now comes the difficult part. Apparently
we also go back into the Garden at death 'by the hinder

---

[1] Lewis distinguishes various different meanings of Genius in *The Allegory
of Love* (1938), 361–3; see also his 'Genius and Genius', *RES*, xii (1936),
189–94, reprinted in his *Studies in Medieval and Renaissance Literature*
(Cambridge, 1966), 169 ff., and D. T. Starnes, 'The Figure Genius in the
Renaissance', *SR*, xi (1964), 234–44.

gate'. There we stay for a long time. Then one of two
things may happen to us: either we are 'clad with other
hew' or else we are 'sent into the chaungefull world
againe'. What can Spenser mean here? Does he intend
to set out a full Buddhist or Theosophical doctrine of
Reincarnation?

The backward view to an existence preceding birth is
in agreement with a stanza in *An Hymne in Honour of
Beautie*:

> For Love is a celestiall harmonie,
> Of likely harts composd of starres concent,
> Which joyne together in sweete sympathie,
> To worke ech others joy and true content,
> Which they have harbourd since their first descent
> Out of their heavenly bowres, where they did see
> And know ech other here belov'd to bee.
>
> (ll. 197–203)

Both passages clearly stem from *Phaedrus* 250–3, where
Plato develops a doctrine of affinities in love. Every lover
looks for qualities in the beloved that remind him of the
god he followed in a former life. They 'keep their eyes
fixed upon the god, and as they reach and grasp him by
memory they are inspired and receive from him character
and habits, so far as it is possible for a man to have part in
God'. As for the forward view to the return to the Garden,
and to alternative destinies (either to be 'clad with other
hew' or sent back into the world), there were some
Neoplatonists of the Renaissance who held a doctrine that
will fit it quite well. Henry More, for example, believed
that after death the human soul becomes an aerial

daemon. When this aerial term is completed, if the
soul makes the grade it becomes an aetherial spirit like
the angels, and is beyond all change. If, however, it fails
to make the grade, it returns into a terrestrial body.[1]

Such doctrines, then, were to be found in the works of
the Platonists. But, granted that, how could Spenser call
himself a Christian and believe in them? Two very different answers to this question occur; and each may in
part be true. The first is that the whole school of thought
to which Spenser belonged felt that in the long run
everything must be reconcilable. There was no belief,
however pagan or bizarre it might seem, that could not be
accommodated somehow, if only it were rightly understood. The other answer is that Spenser may not have
intended the doctrines as articles of belief at all. What
makes me think the Garden is not fully meant as metaphysics is this, that from a formal point of view it exists for
the purpose of defining Amoret as against Belphoebe, the
lover, wife, and mother as against the virgin huntress.[2]
Diana took the one twin into a quasi-divine, unchangeable
life. Venus plunges the other into the world of generation: the world, that is, of pleasure, spontaneity, and
sexuality, but the world also of mutability and chance.

Or try it the other way round, approaching the passage
from the stance we may imagine Spenser to have taken
up as he wrote it. Perhaps his train of thought went

[1] See *The Immortality of the Soul*, esp. III, i, 3–5 and xvii, 15 f.; and cf. Plutarch, *De facie*, 943–5.
[2] It is significant that the passage quoted above from *An Hymne in Honour of Beautie* is not primarily about prenatal life, either. It too is a poem about love.—F.

something like this: I will not give a woman like Amoret any place lower than Belphoebe's, nor value the one life less than the other. Yes, I know Amoret's way is desperately mortal: lovers die, and, worse still, love can die. But don't you see that Amoret herself, in her freshness, her spontaneity, and her innocent voluptuousness, is not merely a symbol but a . . . demonstration of—an ambassadress from—the only power we know that repairs death and secures permanence even for a mutable world? She glows and is fragrant with the same bewitching power that continually imposes new forms of beauty and energy upon brute matter. And you can gauge what esteem that power merits from the fact that our momentary participations in it are the theme of half the world's poetry—or from the fact that it is the source we all came from. This is obviously the case in the sense that our causes lay there. But are you quite sure that we ourselves didn't do the same? Perhaps there is something in the Platonic idea that there was more than we can remember on the far side of the gates of birth, even that the gates of death open on the same region. But I was talking about Amoret . . . [1]

It goes without saying that Amoret's childhood in the Garden and her womanhood in the Temple of Venus are not really two successive stages in a biography. We should think of them, rather, as two co-temporal aspects of the way of life she symbolizes. Thus, the earthly-lovable

[1] A somewhat similar train of thought may be imagined to lie behind the concluding speech of Milton's *Comus*, with its vision of 'happy climes . . . Up in the broad fields of the sky' (997–9). There, too, reposes Adonis 'Waxing well of his deep wound', and there 'th' *Assyrian* Queen' his Venus; with 'farr above'—the indication of level is significant—'Celestial *Cupid*'.

contains, on the one hand, the innocence and spontaneity of the *Anima mundi*; on the other, the breeding, discipline, and civilization of a fine social life, which is itself governed by Venus in the sense of 'a fully human tradition of conscious love'.

5

The foregoing explorations all took their departure, ultimately, from a single image, the statue of the evil Cupid in the House of Busyrane. This prompts a general reflection on the form of *The Faerie Queene*. Its characteristic thickness of texture is not a matter of local complexities (though there are plenty of those), so much as of resonances sounding at large throughout the poem. Widely separated passages may at any time turn out to be interconnected, and the connection will perhaps depend on descriptive details that at first seemed insignificant. Carelessness over such details, therefore, can vitiate far more than the interpretation of the passage immediately concerned. Reading *The Faerie Queene* is like following out the threads of a tapestry so intricately woven that a single mistake may tear the whole fabric.

Yet it is precisely with the descriptive details of the poem that critics are often most careless. As an awful example, take a recent interpretation of the following stanza:

> She having hong upon a bough on high
>   Her bow and painted quiver, had unlaste
>   Her silver buskins from her nimble thigh,
>   And her lancke loynes ungirt, and breasts unbraste,
>   After her heat the breathing cold to taste;

Her golden lockes, that late in tresses bright
Embreaded were for hindring of her haste,
Now loose about her shoulders hong undight,
And were with sweet *Ambrosia* all besprinckled light.

(III, vi, 18)

In an essay in the first volume of the Pelican *Guide to English Literature*, Mr Derek Traversi quotes this stanza as a 'description of Britomart'.[1] It so happens that the figure described is named as Diana only two stanzas earlier. But suppose that Traversi had only the one stanza to go on. We can then distinguish three levels of error in his false identification.

First, we have the simple factual errors. The stanza describes an archer, whereas Britomart, as we know very well from such incidents as her encounter with Guyon at III, i, 5–10, carries lance and sword. The archer wears silver buskins, whereas a great point is made about Britomart's complete armour. (Traversi does not explain how buskins could be combined with full armour.) And the buskined archer's hair is sprinkled with ambrosia, whereas we know Britomart to be mortal. Secondly, we have what may be called iconographical errors. If the stanza had been read rightly, the bow and quiver would have indicated at once that the figure was likely to be Diana, or her foster-child Belphoebe. In distinguishing between these, one might have expected the material of the buskins to be of help. Silver is a Lunar metal, and therefore appropriate for Diana. Belphoebe, on the other hand, is a daughter of the sun, and accordingly wears golden buskins—

[1] 'Spenser's *Faerie Queene*' in *The Age of Chaucer*, ed. Boris Ford (1954), 223.

> gilden buskins of costly Cordwaine,
> All bard with golden bendes...   (II, iii, 27)

But the error goes to a third and far deeper level. Traversi appears to have forgotten the whole myth of Belphoebe and Amoret. For the myth is based throughout on a polar contrast of fertility and virginity, a contrast that is nowhere more obvious than in Amoret's adoption by Venus, Belphoebe's by Diana. Diana and Belphoebe are virgin, Venus and Amoret fertile. If, then, Traversi had to confuse Britomart with either of the goddesses, her destiny as the progenitress of a dynasty (III, iii, 24), not to speak of her portrayal from the outset as one deeply in love, ought to have determined him not on any account to choose Diana.

Consequently, when Traversi finds in the misnamed figure a 'typical' contrast between 'prevailing morality' and 'decorative sensuality', we strongly suspect him of a naïve response to nudity—of assuming that it is a sign, not of the real, the pure, and the natural, but of 'Britomart's' sexiness. When he concludes that 'it is not the allegory that brings the verse to life', we find ourselves muttering 'But how should he know?' And when he advances the generalization that in Spenser 'the evidence of style is too powerful, too immediate to be countered even by contrary assertion',[1] we judge that what he really means must be, 'Any impression made on my mind by a passage, however isolated from its context or attributed to a wrong context, is final'.

[1] *The Age of Chaucer*, 222.

CHAPTER IV

THE IMAGE OF EVIL

I

So far, the images of evil that we have discussed have been solemn, solitary, silent and sterile (as in the House of Busyrane); or bogus, provocative, and inactive (as in the Bower of Bliss); or very expensive (as in both). The images of good, on the other hand, have either been spontaneous, shameless, and fertile, like those of the Garden of Adonis; or ordered, arduous, and active, like those of the Temple of Venus. Let us now consider Spenser's sense of good and evil in general.

But first look at the image of evil as it appears in other poets. In Marlowe, say:

> Nature, that fram'd us of four elements
> Warring within our breasts for regiment,
> Doth teach us all to have aspiring minds:
> Our souls...
> Still climbing after knowledge infinite,
> And always moving as the restless spheres,
> Wills us to wear ourselves and never rest,
> Until we reach the ripest fruit of all,
> The perfect bliss and sole felicity,
> The sweet fruition of an earthly crown.
>
> (*I Tamburlaine*, II, vii, 18–21, 24–9)

These metaphysics of magicians,
And necromantic books are heavenly;
Lines, circles, scenes, letters, and characters;

The Image of Evil

Ay, these are those that Faustus most desires.
O, what a world of profit and delight,
Of power, of honour, of omnipotence,
Is promis'd to the studious artizan!
All things that move between the quiet poles
Shall be at my command: emperors and kings
Are but obey'd in their several provinces,
Nor can they raise the wind, or rend the clouds;
But his dominion that exceeds in this,
Stretcheth as far as doth the mind of man;
A sound magician is a mighty god:
Here, tire my brains to get a deity!

(*Doctor Faustus*, 77–91)

Or Shakespeare:

Hie thee hither,
That I may pour my spirits in thine ear,
And chastise with the valour of my tongue
All that impedes thee from the golden round,
Which fate and metaphysical aid doth seem
To have thee crown'd withal.

Come, you spirits
That tend on mortal thoughts! unsex me here,
And fill me from the crown to the toe top full
Of direst cruelty... (*Macbeth*, I, v, 26–31, 41–4)

Or Milton:

What though the field be lost?
All is not lost; the unconquerable Will,
And study of revenge, immortal hate,
And courage never to submit or yield.

(*Paradise Lost*, i, 105–8)

In all these passages, evil is portrayed as involving immense concentrations of will. Even the much milder and merrier evil of Milton's Comus is spritely and virile:

Rigor now is gon to bed,
And Advice with scrupulous head,
Strict Age, and sowre Severity,
With their grave Saws in slumber ly.
We that are of purer fire
Imitate the Starry Quire.   (*Comus*, 107–12)

He is chuckling and defiant, like a child or a youth:
'We won't go home till morning' is what, in effect, he is
saying. If we had to put it in a word, we would say that
in all three poets evil appears as *energy*—lawless and
rebellious energy, no doubt, but nevertheless energy,
abounding and upsurging. From this, I believe, springs the
difficulty these poets have in making the good a fit
antagonist for the evil. It is why Tamburlaine's victims
are nonentities and Faustus' good angel a mere stick;
why Richmond seems so pale beside Richard III; and
why Milton's God has a popularity rating lower than his
Satan.

When we turn to the image of evil in Spenser, we find
a very noticeable difference. For in *The Faerie Queene* evil
does not usually appear as energy.

Here certain *caveats* should be entered. First, the
difference need imply no distinct doctrinal position. It is
not at all likely to have been the result of conscious philosophizing on Spenser's part. Secondly, full allowance has
to be made for the exigencies of *genre*. For the difference
springs in part simply from the different requirements of
dissimilar forms. Thus, Spenser's concern as an allegorist
is not with the moment of an avaricious choice, but with
the whole life-long state of the avaricious man; not with
the moment of yielding to a particular sexual temptation,

but with the life-long state of the nympholept. But with these *caveats* we may still admit the impression that Spenser has a different vision of the world, and one not, I think, less profound.

2

At least five different forms in which evil appears in *The Faerie Queene* may be distinguished.

First, and least important, are the various paynim knights who appear as momentary enemies. With some of them, it is true, there is something that might at first be taken for energy. One thinks, for example, of the violent approach of Pyrochles, as he comes to attack Guyon. But notice, here, the tendency of the imagery: the single-track concentration on brightness and heat. Pyrochles' 'bright arms' shine like the sun, and

> round about him threw forth sparkling fire,
> That seemd him to enflame on every side.   (II, v, 2)

Even his horse is 'bloody red'. At the conclusion of the encounter the emphasis is, if possible, still more pronounced. Pyrochles runs, still in full armour, into a muddy lake, and with 'raging arms' keeps desperately beating the water. 'I burne, I burne, I burne', he shouts, 'O howe I burne with implacable fire' (II, vi, 44). And he begs Atin to help him to a death that will save him from the invisible flames. As Canto vi ends, he is crying 'These flames, these flames', and repeating over and over again how he burns within with a bright fire which consumes his entrails. What we are seeing is an image not of energy but of agonized frenzy. Everything about Pyrochles—

the brightness, the heat, the reiterations—belongs to a picture of frenetic anguish.

Next, there are images of disease and defect. Defect, for instance, is the keynote of the portrayal of Abessa and Corceca. When Una spoke to Abessa 'the rude wench her answer'd nought at all', for the good reason that 'She could not heare, nor speake, nor understand' (I, iii, 11). She fled in terror,

> And home she came, whereas her mother blynd
> Sate in eternall night: nought could she say,
> But suddaine catching hold, did her dismay
> With quaking hands... (I, iii, 12)

The normal functions are inhibited, impaired, or lacking altogether. In Maleger, on the other hand, it is disease that is more prominent:

> As pale and wan as ashes was his looke,
>   His bodie leane and meagre as a rake,
>   And skin all withered like a dryed rooke,
>   Thereto as cold and drery as a Snake. (II, xi, 22)

His very power lies in his deficiency, so that he is 'most strong in most infirmitee' (II, xi, 40). So with Malbecco, who out of jealousy throws himself off a cliff. The emphasis falls first on fear: 'fearful agony', a rock 'suspended dreadfully' that would 'terrify' anyone; then on a physical lightness (Malbecco falls 'so flit and light' that he is not even hurt) that renders the sensation of being afraid at the same time as it shows the fear baseless; then on fear again,

> continuall feare
> Of that rockes fall... (III, x, 58)

But as vain horror deforms him into Jealousy itself, the imagery is primarily of disease. A diet of toads and frogs

> in his cold complexion do breed
> A filthy bloud, or humour rancorous,
> Matter of doubt and dread suspitious,
> That doth with curelesse care consume the hart,
> Corrupts the stomacke with gall vitious,
> Croscuts the liver with internall smart.   (III, x, 59)

As for the Seven Deadly Sins themselves, every one of them is either diseased or deformed or both. In Sloth 'A shaking fever raignd continually' (I, iv, 20); Gluttony is 'Full of diseases...And a dry dropsie through his flesh did flow' (St. 23); and Luxury suffers from

> that fowle evill, which all men reprove,
> That rots the marrow, and consumes the braine.
>   (I, iv, 26)

Similarly, Avarice is dying of the 'vile disease' of always wanting more, and also has gout; Envy's mouth is leprous; and Anger is afflicted by spleen, raging frenzy, palsy, and St. Francis' fire.

Thirdly, evil may take the form of the disgusting. Such, for example, is the monster Errour, 'most lothsom, filthie, foule'. When St George seized her by the gorge

> she spewd out of her filthy maw
> A floud of poyson horrible and blacke,
> Full of great lumpes of flesh and gobbets raw,
> Which stunck so vildly,[1] that it forst him slacke
> His grasping hold, and from her turne him backe.
>   (I, i, 20)

---

[1] Vilely.

Her vomit (the constituents of which are described) had defiled the whole place. Similarly with Duessa in her exposure by St George and Arthur. 'Her misshaped parts did them appal,' we are told. And no wonder:

> Her teeth out of her rotten gummes were feld,[1]
> And her sowre breath abhominably smeld;
> Her dried dugs, like bladders lacking wind,
> Hong downe, and filthy matter from them weld;
> Her wrizled[2] skin as rough, as maple rind,
> So scabby was, that would have loathd all womankind.
>
> (I, viii, 47)

A fourth and quite different class of images are those in which evil takes the form of a temptation to relax, or to fall asleep, or to die. St George is incapacitated for his encounter with Orgoglio because he has drunk from the enervating fountain of sloth, 'that fraile fountaine, which him feeble made' (I, vii, 11). His mistake was to sit down beside it to rest, just as the nymph of the fountain herself had done, when she was supposed to be engaged in the arduous pursuits of Diana.[3] With Phaedria, the temptation is to fall quite asleep. Her song about the fruitlessness of labour is a lullaby, which charms Cymochles, while he lies with his head 'disarmed In her loose lap', until he slumbers, caring about 'no worldly thing' (II, vi, 14–18). The sirens' song to Guyon at II, xii, 30–3 falls into the same category. But in the heavier temptation of Despayre we hear the death-wish itself, which underlies this whole form of evil. He invites St George to 'enjoy eternall rest

[1] Broken.　　　　　　　　[2] Wrinkled.
[3] Hence the origin of the fountain, as Spenser explains at I, vii, 4f. Angry because the nymph sat down 'in middest of the race', Diana made her waters dull and slow too; so that 'all that drunke thereof, did faint and feeble grow'.

And happie ease' (I, ix, 40)—an invitation that is grounded on a subtle perversion of the ideal of resignation:

> Is not his deed, what ever thing is donne,
>> In heaven and earth? did not he all create
>> To die againe? all ends that was begonne.
>> Their times in his eternall booke of fate
>> Are written sure, and have their certaine date.
>> Who then can strive with strong necessitie,
>> That holds the world in his still chaunging state,
>> Or shunne the death ordaynd by destinie?
> When houre of death is come, let none aske whence, nor why.
>
> (I, ix, 42)

Fifthly and finally, there is the Waste House. This form of evil, which is often the most elaborately developed by Spenser, had its classic expression in Virgil's hell, where Aeneas goes *perque domos Ditis vacuas et inania regna*.[1] We have already met the type, in the House of Busyrane. For that house, with its magnificence in room after room, its silence, and its desertion, is undoubtedly a place of death. Britomart marvels at the décor,

> But more she mervaild that no footings trace,
> Nor wight appear'd, but wastefull emptinesse,
> And solemne silence over all that place
>
> . . . .
>
> Thus she there waited untill eventyde,
> Yet living creature none she saw appeare.
>
> (III, xi, 53–5)

Another instance is the House of Orgoglio. When Arthur forces an entry

> living creature none he did espye;
> Then gan he lowdly through the house to call:

---

[1] 'Through the empty halls of Dis and his vacant realm' (*Aen.* vi, 269).

> But no man car'd to answere to his crye.
> There raignd a solemne silence over all,
> Nor voice was heard, nor wight was seene in bowre
>   or hall.   (I, viii, 29)

Eventually a feeble old man comes tottering out: Ignaro, Orgoglio's foster-father. To question after question he replies that 'he could not tell'. He lives in the oppressor's house, but knows nothing about what is going on, knows nothing of a prisoner, knows nothing. Arthur, seeing that the old man is senile, borrows his keys and searches the castle. Again, as in the House of Busyrane, there is everywhere great richness: 'royal arras and resplendent gold' fit for the greatest prince. Arthur at last calls with his whole power, through a little grating in an iron door. And from the dungeon within comes a voice 'hollow, dreary, murmuring', the voice of St George.

In the Cave of Mammon the richness is naturally given more prominence. But it is plain enough that here again we have to do with a Waste House. Mammon himself is dressed in rusty iron and in gold obscured with dust; and his riches are accumulations of wealth 'that never could be spent' (II, vii, 4 f.). It is a place of death, whose entry, descending into the hollow ground, lies next the gate of hell. At this point there comes a strange detail, something finer than the allegorical. Before the gate of hell and the door of Richesse there sits an unusual Harpy:

> sad *Celeno*, sitting on a clift,
> A song of bale and bitter sorrow sings,
> That hart of flint a sunder could have rift.
>   (II, vii, 23)

The Image of Evil

Why this pathos at the entry to the house of Mammon? There is no simple answer to be given in terms of allegory. The house itself is a huge cave with stalactites of gold, but all covered with cobwebs and soot. Roof, floor, walls: all are gold; but gold 'overgrowne with dust and old decay' (St. 29). There have been so many images of decay and neglect that it is not a great surprise when we come to the bones of unburied men, lying scattered about. Yet the house does not lack the wherewithal for burial. It has a garden of poisonous fruits, of black plants 'Fit to adorne the dead, and decke the drery toombe' (St. 51).

Surveying all five forms, we notice a distinction observed by Spenser that seems in part to have governed his choice of the form evil takes in any particular instance. When figures representing evils speak to human characters—that is, tempt them—they may express either the sleep-wish (the lighter form) or the death-wish (the heavier). But in the narrative parts of the poem, when we ourselves are looking at the evils from outside their world, they appear either as filth, defect, disease (the lighter form) or as life-in-death, a silent, empty imprisonment, 'dust and old decay' (the heavier). In no instance, however, is evil ever represented as upsurging energy.

CHAPTER V

MUTABILITY

Or rather, in no instance but one. For the Titaness Mutabilitie would appear to be an exception. But the *Cantos of Mutabilitie* are a very special case: Spenser is there playing a very subtle, not to say dangerous, game. And, anyway, Mutabilitie is not of course a vice in the ordinary sense. She represents a cosmic principle, which in certain respects may be compared to the principle known to our own science as entropy.

The drama of Mutabilitie is set out in two acts. In the first she certainly is, or appears to be, an evil figure. Like the goddess of war,

> So likewise did this *Titanesse* aspire,
>   Rule and dominion to her selfe to gaine.
>
> (VII, vi, 4)

On earth, first, she destroyed the 'good estate' and 'meet order' that Nature had established. And not content with breaking natural law, she

> wrong of right, and bad of good did make,
> And death for life exchanged foolishlie:
> Since which, all living wights have learn'd to die,
> And all this world is woxen daily worse.
> O pittious worke of *MUTABILITIE*!
> By which, we all are subject to that curse,
> And death in stead of life have sucked from our Nurse.
>
> (VII, vi, 6)

Next, Mutabilitie proceeds to assert her rule over the

planets. (This manifestation of mutability would seem in Spenser's time a matter of obvious fact.) Her first victory is to produce an eclipse of the moon, which arouses a fear

> least *Chaos* broken had his chaine,
> And brought againe on them eternall night.
>
> (vii, vi, 14)

This all looks very black; but soon there is a hint that Mutabilitie has also a more favourable aspect. In the sphere of Jupiter the gods

> gave good eare
> To her bold words, and marked well her grace,
> Beeing of stature tall as any there
> Of all the Gods, and beautifull of face,
> As any of the Goddesses in place.   (vii, vi, 28)

And when Jupiter makes to dispose of her with a thunder-bolt, he cannot bring himself to do it. She is too beautiful: 'Such sway doth beauty even in Heaven beare' (St. 31). What is most surprising of all, Mutabilitie questions Jupiter's impartiality, and goes over his head—

> to the highest him, that is behight
> Father of Gods and men by equall might;
> To weet, the God of Nature, I appeale. (vii, vi, 35)

She proceeds, notice, in a perfectly constitutional manner, by taking her case to a higher court.

The second act is entirely devoted to the trial. God appears as judge, but of course in the person of his Vicegerent Nature, and even she is veiled. Yet in spite of this double concealment of the divine, Nature's robe has an effect on the viewer like that of the robe of the Transfiguration, it is 'so bright and wondrous sheene' (vII, vii, 7). In keeping with this animating presence, the whole trial scene is marked by tremendous richness and majesty, order and spontaneity. Mutabilitie, to prove her case and so to rule the universe, produces the greatest of all the poem's pageants. She calls as her witnesses the Seasons and Months, Day and Night, the Hours, and Life and Death, in all their incessant interchange. It is persuasive. But the more Mutabilitie proves her case, the more she refutes it. For it is precisely in the pattern of continual mutation that the permanence of Nature consists. And this, by a swift but inevitable-seeming *peripeteia*, is Dame Nature's verdict. She adds one thing: a warning to Mutabilitie to accept her ruling and aspire no further, 'For thy decay thou seekst by thy desire' (vII, vii, 59). In demanding absolute mutability the Titaness seeks her own decay, since the assent to that demand must end the permanence of Nature. Nature once gone, mutability will indeed be complete—there will be no more mutability, no more change of any kind: 'thenceforth, none no more change shall see'.

The whole debate is thus revealed to be another *coincidentia oppositorum*. Change and permanence when carried up to the cosmic level are not really opposed, but involve one another. Both exist now in mutual dependence; and both, one day, will be annihilated. For Nature is merely an exposition of the *natura unialis*. Of that, her verdict at the trial shows her to be well aware:

> But time shall come that all shall changed bee,
> And from thenceforth, none no more change shall see.
>
> (vII, vii, 59)

No sooner has this been said than we see it happen, emblematically:

> Then was that whole assembly quite dismist,
> And *Natur's* selfe did vanish, whither no man wist.

After that we have only Spenser's own voice, praying for eternity in the two stanzas of the imperfect Eighth Canto. So far as we know, he had no intention of ending *The Faerie Queene* at this point. But has any poem ever had a better end?

These, then, are the two acts into which the drama of the *Mutabilitie Cantos* is divided. In between Act I and Act II, however, there is interposed, of all things, a comic interlude. It is the story of Faunus, a 'foolish god', who gets one of Diana's nymphs to help him see her mistress with no clothes on. Spenser handles the story with a very light touch. Notice, for example, the detached, ironic effect of the feminine rhymes in the one stanza where Faunus speaks, corrupting the nymph Molanna. But at the same time there are overtones of a meaning far more deeply intended. When Faunus gets his wish and sees Diana naked, he betrays himself by his inability to maintain a reverent silence in the presence of divine beauty. Instead, his response is a guffaw:

> There *Faunus* saw that pleased much his eye,
>   And made his hart to tickle in his brest,
>   That for great joy of some-what he did spy,
>   He could him not containe in silent rest;
>   But breaking forth in laughter, loud profest
>   His foolish thought. A foolish *Faune* indeed,
>   That couldst not hold thy selfe so hidden blest,

Spenser's Images of Life

But wouldest needs thine owne conceit areed.[1]
Babblers unworthy been of so divine a meed. (vii, vi, 46)

The simile that compares Diana to a housewife who has caught an animal drinking milk in her dairy returns to a homely pastoral anthropomorphism. Yet it encourages us, also, to think of Faunus as representing a merely natural level of existence, altogether beneath that of Diana.

Never was Spenser closer to the Italian painters than here. Compare, for example, the mood of Botticelli's *Mars and Venus*. It is by no means that of a sensual love-scene. The impression imparted is rather of a profoundly felt statement that the spirit of love can and should pacify strife. The face of the Venus, in particular, expresses grave serenity and peace, as much as any sexual feeling. Certainly its emotional tenor is deeply serious. Yet, in between the heads of the principals, and apparently oblivious to their high destiny, are three entirely comic fauns playing with Mars' armour.

In its effect, therefore, the fable of Faunus turns out not to be an interlude after all, but a countermovement in the main action. For in Canto vi we see Nature in what now emerge as two opposed aspects. First, we see her in her grandeur, represented by the planetary deities. Secondly, we see her in her grotesque, naïve manifestations, represented by local and ridiculous deities. Finally, in the Seventh Canto, we see her herself, in the union of her opposites, so far at least as her veil allows.

[1] I.e. 'But had to express your own idea.'

78

CHAPTER VI

THE IMAGE OF GOOD

I

The mention of Nature's veils leads to my next topic, the poem's expositions of good. For the first thing we notice about the Spenserian images of good is their veiled, mysterious, even hidden, character. To start with, they are withheld altogether. For they do not really begin until the third canto of the poem. By then we have already had several images of evil: Errour, Archimago and his spirits, the separation of Una and St George with everything that that implies, and finally Duessa. All this time, Una has kept her face hidden. For when she was first described, in the opening stanzas of the poem, she rode

> Upon a lowly Asse more white then snow,
> Yet she much whiter, but the same did hide
> Under a vele, that wimpled was full low. (I, i, 4)

Now that she is alone and in distress, she wanders through deserted wildernesses, searching for St George. But here, one day,

> From her unhastie beast she did alight,
> And on the grasse her daintie limbes did lay
> In secret shadow, farre from all mens sight:
> From her faire head her fillet she undight,
> And laid her stole aside. Her angels face
> As the great eye of heaven shyned bright,
> And made a sunshine in the shadie place. (I, iii, 4)

The first image of good reveals itself with brilliant effect.

The secret and voluntary unveiling of Truth stands in direct contrast to the public and enforced unmasking of Falsehood. In the Eighth Canto Duessa is openly stripped of her borrowed robes by Arthur and St George, so that

> her borrowed light
> Is laid away, and counterfesaunce[1] knowne.   (I, viii, 49)

As for the remote locality of Una's unveiling—'In secret shadow, farre from all mens sight' (I, iii, 4)—it is to recur more than once as a condition for the appearance of good. Thus Belphoebe ranges the wild forest; Arthur takes Serena to a 'little Hermitage' which lies 'Far from all neighbourhood, the which annoy it may' (VI, v, 34); and the place where Calidore sees the Graces is 'far from all peoples tread' (VI, x, 5).

After the Third Canto, Una never unveils again, until she is in her father's castle being betrothed to St George. Then she lays aside the stole and wimple that hid her beauty during the book's journey, and puts on a robe of spotless white. And now for the first time the blazing beams of her gloriously beautiful face shine fully on St George. The human soul, married to Truth *in patria*, at last sees her clearly. In spite of all the earlier partial glimpses, the vision is amazing:

> her owne deare loved knight,
> All were she dayly with himselfe in place,
> Did wonder much at her celestiall sight.
>
> (I, xii, 23)

As we have seen, the characteristic of being veiled is shared by other Spenserian images of good. Venus and

---

[1] Deception.

Nature themselves are in this life seen only under veils. And the Graces, who appear not only unveiled but totally naked, are an exception that proves the rule, since they disappear altogether when an uninitiated mortal surprises them (VI, x, 18).

Throughout the poem, indeed, veiling and unveiling are actions of key significance. Here I include the putting-on and removal of armour, whose function is often, at least in part, that of a mask (thus Archimago rides disguised as St George, wearing armour like his 'the person to put on'[1]). When Britomart disarms, she is suddenly revealed as a woman of divine beauty, to the wonder of Satyrane and Paridell, who gaze at her 'in contemplation of divinity' and in admiration of her nobility (III, ix, 20ff.). Similarly, a later removal of her helmet, this time accidental, gives Artegall his first sight of her face, and makes him kneel before her 'Weening some heavenly goddesse he did see' (IV, vi, 19ff.). But if the unveiling of the good leads to immediate respect and reverence, it is quite the reverse with the evil. A false Florimell may deceive everyone until she is confronted with the true; but then

> Streight way so soone as both together met,
> Th' enchaunted Damzell vanisht into nought:
> Her snowy substance melted as with heat,
> Ne of that goodly hew remaynèd ought,
> But th'emptie girdle, which about her wast was
>   wrought.[2]

[1] I, ii, 11; cf. I, iii, 24ff.
[2] v, iii, 24. Florimell herself, however, is only relatively genuine. To Arthur, who is always seeking Gloriana without knowing exactly what she is like,

In any fair comparison with the genuine, the false is instantly unmasked and discredited, its illusion dispelled.

The effect of this frequent veiling and unveiling is to make us distrustful of outward show. We are constantly kept awake to the deceptiveness of the forms of life— to the complex difference between appearance and reality. This effect is silently corroborated at a hundred points by a feature of the pageants that has already been discussed. I mean the peculiarity that while the pageants are self-explanatory to us they are utterly cryptic to the characters within the fiction. Thus the poem all the time and in many different ways expresses Spenser's deep sense 'that in this world things are not truly but in equivocal shapes'.[1]

The good may appear, then, as Fact. It is genuine, it is real, and it is (usually) hidden.

2

A moment after her unveiling in the wilderness of despair and exile Una is at first frightened then comforted by, of all things, a lion. When it sees her it runs at her greedily, but then stops in amazement; for 'the lion will not touch the true prince'.[2] Then

> he kist her wearie feet,
> And lickt her lilly hands with fawning tong,
> As he her wronged innocence did weet.[3]   (I, iii, 6)

Florimell is no more than a 'semblant vain' of his true goal. He follows the (true) Florimell under an illusion:

> Oft did he wish, that Lady faire mote bee
> His Faery Queene, for whom he did complaine.   (III, iv, 54)

We can almost trace a regular sequence of orders of reality, of the form FALSE FLORIMELL : TRUE FLORIMELL : : TRUE FLORIMELL : GLORIANA. See p. 135 below.

[1] Sir Thomas Browne, *Relig. Med.* i, 12.

[2] *I Henry IV*, II, iv, 304.   [3] Know, perceive.

The Image of Good

The lion becomes her faithful companion and a perfect instrument of her will:

> Still when she slept, he kept both watch and ward,
> And when she wakt, he waited diligent,
> With humble service to her will prepard:
> From her faire eyes he tooke commaundement,
> And ever by her lookes conceived her intent.   (i, iii, 9)

Here we have the first statement, in this case mythical, of a theme that is to be sustained throughout *The Faerie Queene*. The lion is a type of the natural, the ingenuous, the untaught: the humble creature that goes right without knowing, or hardly knowing, what it does. It licked Una's hands *as if* it knew her wronged innocence.

The theme is stated again in the Sixth Canto, where Una is rescued from Sansloy by the fauns and satyrs. Again Una is in distress; again she receives grim unlikely-looking assistance (not in this case a lion, but wild wood-gods compared with a lion at i, vi, 10); and again she at first stands in dread of her rescuers. But what this scene adds to the previous one is jocundity and jollity. When Una is reassured,

> So from the ground she fearelesse doth arise,
> And walketh forth without suspect of crime:
> They all as glad, as birdes of joyous Prime,[1]
> Thence lead her forth, about her dauncing round,
> Shouting, and singing all a shepheards ryme.
>
> . . . .
>
> And all the way their merry pipes they sound,
>   That all the woods with doubled Eccho ring,
>   And with their horned feet do weare the ground,
>   Leaping like wanton kids in pleasant Spring. (i, vi, 13 f.)

[1] Spring.

Notice how the episode exalts Una. Far from showing prudery, she recognizes the essential innocence of these rude creatures. After the first tense moment there is a steadily increasing relief. This is, indeed, the first full relaxation in the whole poem. From our present point of view the episode is an important one, because it shows good as fun, as a romp. It may also throw some light as far as the problem of the comic interlude between the two acts of the drama of Mutabilitie. For Spenser, the transition from the planetary deities to the high court of Nature is not unfittingly a relaxation of tension: a *scherzo* movement.

For a later instance of the theme we may turn to the Salvage Man who serves and guards Serena much as the lion did Una. He is so 'salvage' as to be almost sub-human. For example, he has no language but a confused murmur of 'senselesse words, which nature did him teach' (VI, iv, 11). All the same, he did

> His best endevour, and his daily paine,
> In seeking all the woods both farre and nye
> For herbes to dresse their wounds; still seeming faine,
> When ought he did, that did their lyking gaine.
>
> (VI, iv, 16)

In fact, he is a faithful Man Friday to Serena and Calepine. The Wild Man is not always, of course, so helpful a figure. We meet a different sort of savages altogether in the Eighth Canto: cannibals, who very nearly kill Serena as a sacrifice to their dark gods. For with Spenser the Savage is in itself an ambivalent image. On the one

84

hand, what is savage is unreclaimed and bestial; on the other, it is unspoiled and innocent.

Less primitive, but hardly less innocent, are the shepherds of Book VI. With them we have the same sense of jocundity and of relief as we had with the wood-gods who rescued Una. It almost seems as if Spenser shared this feeling; for when he turns to the story of the shepherds at the beginning of the Ninth Canto, the transition reflects more than usual enthusiasm:

> Now turne againe my teme thou jolly swayne,
>   Backe to the furrow which I lately left;
>   I lately left a furrow, one or twayne
>   Unplough'd, the which my coulter hath not cleft:
>   Yet seem'd the soyle both fayre and frutefull eft,[1]
>   As I it past, that were too great a shame,
>   That so rich frute should be from us bereft.

(VI, ix, 1)

The hint here of personal identification tells us a good deal about Spenser. For the shepherds' society that he portrays so attractively is a type of innocent community, of the simple life that anyone may share if he will. As Meliboe says to Calidore,

>   if ye algates[2] covet to assay
>   This simple sort of life, that shepheards lead,
>   Be it your owne: our rudenesse to your selfe aread.[3]

(VI, ix, 33)

When Calidore first comes among the shepherds, he inquires after the Blatant Beast, but learns that in this alone of human societies the Beast is unknown. And at once this innocence is exemplified by the easy hospitality

---

[1] Afterwards.   [2] Altogether.   [3] Adjudge; teach.

with which Calidore is offered food and drink and a place among the admirers of Pastorella. He sits on, with no inclination ever to leave, among flocks feeding and lovers singing—'How sweet is the Shepherd's sweet lot!'[1]

Good may be portrayed as the ingenuous, more or less unconscious, unspoiled, and humble. It is often accompanied by gaiety and fun.

3

The House of Coelia seems at first sight to present a totally different image of good from the ones we have been discussing. There is a good deal about the order and ceremony of the house (a reminder that Spenser was an Elizabethan), and there is much harsh penance to be done. When we look more closely, however, we find that here order itself brings relief and refreshment. The porter at the door of the house, moreover, is Humiltà (I, x, 5), so that we have at least one definite point of resemblance with the previous class of images. Or consider Coelia's hospitality, and the physical relief and relaxation it brings to Una and St George:

> Then called she a Groome, that forth him led
> Into a goodly lodge, and gan despoile
> Of puissant armes, and laid in easie bed;
> His name was meeke *Obedience* rightfully ared. (I, x, 17)

Offsetting the order, in any case, is an equal emphasis on fertility. During the visit, Charissa leaves her 'fruitfull nest' after her latest confinement. She is a bountiful and beautiful woman in her prime, whose

---

[1] William Blake, 'The Shepherd', in *Songs of Innocence*.

>   necke and breasts were ever open bare,
>   That ay thereof her babes might sucke their fill;
>   The rest was all in yellow robes arayed still.
>
>   A multitude of babes about her hong,
>   Playing their sports...   (I, x, 30 f.)

Or take a house that is in some ways even more austere: the hermitage Arthur brings Timias and Serena to, at VI, v, 34. Compare this, which is an exposition of good, with the hermitage of Archimago in I, i, 34 f. Necessarily, they must be very alike. Each is in a lonely place; each is a lowly building; each has a chapel adjacent, where 'holy things' (services) are duly said. But notice the distinctive features Spenser chooses to add in the case of the good hermitage. The good hermit entertains, offering homely fare, it is true, but with 'entire affection'. Archimago, on the other hand, offers nothing at all; his guests look for no entertainment 'where none was: Rest is their feast' (I, i, 35). More striking is the external description of the good hermitage:

>   And nigh thereto a little Chappell stoode,
>   Which being all with Yvy overspred,
>   Deckt all the roofe, and shadowing the roode,
>   Seem'd like a grove faire braunched over hed.
>
>   . . . .
>
>   Small was his house, and like a little cage,
>   For his owne turne, yet inly neate and clene,
>   Deckt with greene boughes, and flowers gay beseene.
>   (VI, v, 35, 38)

The *cage* image is soon explained, when we are told in the following canto that the hermit retired to the hermitage after a lifetime of chivalric service among the dangers and chances of the world. Now he lives alone 'like careless bird in cage'.[1] The repeated images of greenery give a strong conviction of growth and natural vigour. As with Coelia's house, the good life is shown as explicitly a life of religion. But the rider is silently added that for all its chastity it is fertile, and for all its austerity, a kind of liberation—even of snugness.

In the conclusion of the story of Una and St George there is a similarly mingled presentation. Again the order, the formal conduct, is prominent. It is, after all, a ceremonial occasion. As soon as the sentry sees by the early morning light the 'last deadly smoke' go up from the dying dragon, he reports to Una's parents (I, xii, 2). Trumpets sound a triumph. Then all the people come out 'as in solemn feast': the king and queen 'in antique robes'; peers 'gravely gowned'; and youths bearing branches of laurel (Sts. 4 f.). They do solemn obeisance before St George.

But if there is order, it is order of a life-giving kind. Throughout the canto, indeed, the theme of Order is entwined with that of Fertility; for the ceremony is a betrothal, and a betrothal that is to be treated as all but marriage—'the holy knots... That none but death for ever can divide' (St. 37). Immediately after the grave and sober part of the procession that welcomes St George come the girls 'all dauncing in a row'. They are wearing garlands—

> As fresh as flowres in medow greene do grow,
> When morning deaw upon their leaves doth light:
> And in their hands sweet Timbrels all upheld on hight.
>
> (I, xii, 6)

---

[1] VI, vi, 4. Cf. Shakespeare, *King Lear*, v, iii, 9: 'We two alone will sing like birds i' the cage.'

The Image of Good

—and they are compared to Diana's nymphs, some wrestling, some running, some bathing. And after them—no, before, for they push in in front—come the 'fry' of children with 'their wanton sports'. (One recalls the satyrs 'leaping like wanton kids' as they take Una to Sylvanus at I, vi, 14.) Una is crowned, but 'twixt earnest and twixt game' (St. 8). Next, a crowd fearfully inspects the dragon, one anxious mother scolding her child for playing with the talons. It is a frankly comic, almost Chaucerian, interlude.

Just as the comic interlude of Faunus ushered in the appearance of Nature in the *Mutabilitie Cantos*, so now we move to the decisive betrothal ceremony that clinches the action of the whole book. The intervention of Archimago and Duessa is resisted, the banns are renewed, and the sacred rites are solemnized. After the betrothal ceremony itself, however, there is again a touch of antique pagan fertility. They light the epithalamic lamp, 'sprinkle all the posts with wine',[1] and perfume everything, until 'all the house did sweat'. But then at once an explicitly Christian image is added:

> there was an heavenly noise
> Heard sound through all the Pallace pleasantly,
> Like as it had bene many an Angels voice,
> Singing before th' eternall majesty,
> In their trinall triplicities on hye.   (I, xii, 39)

[1] I, xii, 38; cf. *Epithalamion*, 253–6:

> And sprinkle all the postes and wals with wine,
> That they may sweat, and drunken be withall.
> Crowne ye God Bacchus with a coronall,
> And Hymen also crowne with wreathes of vine.

Juxtapositions such as this are highly characteristic of Spenser's manner. His penchant for them is of course a trait that he has in part derived from the pageant sources of his poem. Thus, in a pageant performed at the 1461 Entry of Edward IV into Bristol, the slaying of the dragon was greeted with 'a great melody of angels'.[1] But the untroubled transition from festal jocundity to the angelic hierarchies is also in a deeper and a more general sense characteristic of Spenser's world. It is a world he shared with the earlier Italian painters, a world that Raphael, perhaps, killed for art, and Milton for poetry.[2]

In the Garden of Adonis, order is still more prominently combined with spontaneity and fecundity. The number of shapes bred there may be infinite, yet

> every sort is in a sundry bed
> Set by it selfe, and ranckt in comely rew.

> (iii, vi, 35)

On the other hand, this order is entirely spontaneous. It is organic and intrinsic, reached by doing what is natural:

> Ne needs there Gardiner to set, or sow,
>   To plant or prune: for of their owne accord
>   All things, as they created were, doe grow.

> (iii, vi, 34)

The same interplay of opposites, displayed now in the forms of human society, is found in the Temple of Venus. It is a place of order, even of ordeals; yet 'therein thou-

---

[1] MS Lambeth 306, fol. 132, printed in F. J. Furnivall, *Political, Religious, and Love Poems*, E. E. T. S. xv (1903), 5: 'There was seynt George on horsbakke uppone a tent fyghtyng with a dragone, And the kyng and the quene on hyghe in a castelle, And his doughter benethe with a lambe. And atte the sleyng of the dragone there was a greet melody of aungellys.'

[2] A side-note here reads: 'When I was a boy first wallowing'.—F.

sand payres of lovers walkt' (IV, x, 25). And, if Cupid is absent, still the little loves flutter round Venus 'playing heavenly toyes' (St. 42).

On Mount Acidale Order, Unveiling, and Jocundity are all present together, and all at maximum intensity. Order here becomes almost geometrical, so that the grouping is sharply defined as a pair of concentric circles. Calidore sees a hundred girls dancing 'all raunged in a ring'; inside there are three others dancing and singing; and in the middle of these three, marking the centre of the whole array, is Colin Clout's mistress. Spenser himself compares the beauty of the dancers to that of stars in their celestial dance. It resembles the beauty of Ariadne's crown, which

> is unto the starres an ornament,
> Which round about her move in order excellent.
>
> (VI, x, 13)

Unveiledness is no less at a height; for the hundred and four girls are totally naked. This nakedness, as Colin explains, is symbolic: they

> naked are, that without guile
> Or false dissemblaunce all them plaine may see,
> Simple and true from covert malice free. (VI, x, 24)

As for the jocundity of the scene, when Calidore approaches he hears 'the merry sound' of a pipe, and 'many feete fast thumping th'hollow ground' 'Full merrily, and making gladfull glee'. And Colin the 'jolly shepherd' pipes 'so merrily, as never none'.[1] All this takes place,

---

[1] VI, x, 10 and 15. We recall the merry pipes of the satyrs who 'with their horned feet do wear the ground' (I, vi, 14). Contrast Milton, *Comus*, 173, where it is Comus and his rout who have the 'jocond Flute'.

however, in secret. When we and Calidore intrude, it vanishes, and leaves only the poet, who breaks his pipe with displeasure.

Finally, in the *Mutabilitie Cantos* the themes we have been tracing emerge into almost complete consciousness. Order is here personified. At Nature's court such a plenitude of creatures attend that Arlo can scarce contain them:

> So full they filled every hill and Plaine:
> And had not *Natures* Sergeant (that is *Order*)
> Them well disposed by his busie paine,
> And raunged farre abroad in every border,
> They would have caused much confusion and disorder.
>
> (VII, vii, 4)

Spontaneity cannot be explicitly named like Order; yet it defines itself in the response of all that is subject to Nature. Her pavilion is

> Not such as Craftes-men by their idle skill
> Are wont for Princes states to fashion:
> But th'earth her self of her owne motion,
> Out of her fruitfull bosome made to growe
> Most dainty trees; that, shooting up anon,
> Did seeme to bow their bloosming heads full lowe,
> For homage unto her...
>
> And all the earth far underneath her feete
> Was dight with flowres, that voluntary grew.
>
> (VII, vii, 8, 10)

Then in the great pageant of Mutabilitie's witnesses the opposites are restated. The witnesses are called by Order, the sergeant of the court, but they have spontaneity enough to give evidence of universal mutability. They

teem changefully, yet they constantly work their perfection by fate.

Here the theme of Jocundity receives its fullest expression. It is 'lusty' Spring with his thousand singing birds,
and 'jolly' Summer, while even Autumn 'joyed in his
plentious store' (vii, vii, 30). Among the Months the
emphasis is more striking. April is 'wanton as a Kid';
June is 'jolly' (Sts. 33, 35). An October 'full of merry
glee', tipsy with the wine that 'made him so frollick and
so full of lust', is succeeded by a November who 'took no
small delight' in planting, and a December who made
'merry feasting', gladdened by the memory of his
Saviour's birth (Sts. 39–41). As for May,

> Lord! how all creatures laught, when her they spide,
> And leapt and daunc't as they had ravisht beene!
>
> (vii, vii, 34)

4

What we have been examining is not so much Spenser's
conception as his *sense* of good and evil. We have seen
that evil, as he imagines and imitates it, is pompous
and flashy and expensive, like the House of Pride, or
Orgoglio and Duessa, or the House of Malecasta. Good,
on the contrary, is humble, unconscious, and spontaneous,
and may be inarticulate, naïve, and clumsy—like the
shepherds, the satyrs, and the lion. Or, again, the image
of evil is maimed, diseased, and tormented, like Errour,
the Seven Deadly Sins, Abessa and Corceca, Malbecco,
and the masque of Cupid. But good is embodied in the
superb vitality of a Belphoebe, in the rapturous embrace
of Amoret and Scudamour, and in countless images of

teeming plenitude. It multiplies alike in the natural fecundity of the Garden of Adonis and in the supernatural fecundity of Charissa. Even a good hermit's chapel is in process of turning into a grove.

Good and evil are also diametrically opposed in respect of activity. Normally, it is the image of good that is active. True, evil will sometimes be engaged in hard labour, as Mammon's smiths are ('And every one did swincke,[1] and every one did sweat': II, vii, 36), or the smiths in the House of Care who never rest (IV, v, 36). More usually, however, evil is shown as the suspension of all activity. One thinks of the Bower where no one makes love; or the endless empty silences of Orgoglio's castle and the House of Busyrane; or the dusty cobwebbed unused caves of Mammon; or the immobility of Despayre in his dark cave musing.

In direct contrast both to the labour of evil and to its inactivity is the energy of the image of good. Sometimes, good is painful and penitential, as at the House of Coelia. But far more often it is a matter of knightly quests, of dances, revels, and love-making, of 'skipping like wanton kids', of romping. Consequently, whereas evil places tend to be empty or thinly populated, good places are full of figures in joyous motion. The only instance I can recall of an image of good encouraging inactivity is soon recognized to be the exception that proves the rule. When Una's father hears the story of St George's adventures, his response is compassionate. Speaking with sensible logic he advises relaxation, so that for one

[1] Labour.

moment we hear a good voice express something like
the sentiments of the Sirens, or of Despayre:

> But since now safe ye seised have the shore,
> And well arrived are, (high God be blest)
> Let us devize of ease and everlasting rest.   (i, xii, 17)

And what he says might be right; for there must be a true
as well as a false rest. All the same, the invitation is
immediately rejected by St George. His faith binds him
not to rest, but to return to the Faerie Queen for further
service.

In sum, then, evil is solemn, good is gay. Evil means
starvation, good glows with what Blake calls 'the lineaments of gratified desire'.[1] Evil imprisons, good sets free.
Evil is tired, good is full of vigour. The one says, Let go,
lie down, sleep, die; the other, All aboard! kill the dragon,
marry the girl, blow the pipes and beat the drum, let
the dance begin.[2]

Spenser writes in the Letter to Ralegh that *The Faerie
Queene* allegorizes the twelve virtues of Aristotle. But
this is quite an unimportant aspect of the poem. In actual
fact what Spenser has done is to make an image of the
whole of life, a hymn to the universe that he and his

[1] *Gnomic Verses*, xvii, 4.

[2] A cancelled passage here reads: 'The deepest thing *The Faerie Queene* is
saying lies somewhere between two maxims, the one a bit above it, the other a
bit below. 1. *Habe caritatem et fac quod vis.* 2. Rabelais i 57 [the chapter about
the Rule of the Thelemites: 'Do what you will']. The famous fart.

'All this connected with the mediaeval delight in...' Lewis seems here
to have been sketching out a formulation of his views about the limita-
tions of the world of *The Faerie Queene* (cf. the passage at p. 140 below).
Spenser's unmoralistic affirmation of life is higher than a mere tolerance of
irregularities, but on the other hand it does not quite attain a religious vision
of a way transcending morality.—F.

contemporaries believed themselves to inhabit. This also was what certain of the Italian painters did. For the universe, as they conceived it, is a great dance or ceremony or society. It is Chalcidius' *caelestis chorea* and Alanus' cosmic city of which Earth is a suburb. They believed, too, that our virtue and happiness here and now lie in participating in this ceremony as much as we can. Hereafter, we shall do so more fully.

Thus, while the world is for Spenser a place as dangerous and as cryptic or equivocal as the forests of his poem, yet joy and revelry are the core of it. Anywhere in this wood you may meet that joy, veiled or perhaps unveiled. Anywhere you may hear angels singing—or come upon satyrs romping. What is more, the satyrs may lead you to the angels. For Spenser has no Counter-Reformation or classical scruples. He never reaches, yet in a way it is his glory never to reach, that form of the sublime which excludes the homely.

Obviously Spenser's world is very different from the world of Shakespeare, in which evil so often appears as terrific energy. But this difference should not be exaggerated into a clear philosophical disagreement. For one thing, Spenser is not really philosophizing about the inactivity of evil.[1] This is a feature that emerges in his poem whether he will or no; his conscious philosophizing is a smaller matter. For another, we have to allow for the differences of form. Shakespeare presents stories in which the actions themselves are real and significant.

[1] Perhaps an overstatement. The inactivity of evil in Spenser's universe seems at least a distinctively Neoplatonic feature.—F.

He shows men acting, with lust or hatred or ambition as the spur of their action. And of course at the moment of action the evil motive is an energy, a force *moving* them to action. Spenser, however, is only superficially a narrative poet. He is much more concerned with the state of being a good or a bad man, than with the actions by which we become so. In his 'bad' places 'the poet gives us, not merely images of the baits to sin, but much more pictures of the mental atmosphere in which the sinner is entrapped'.[1] We may add, And in his good places, pictures of the large room into which the good man is liberated. He shows us not what it is like to murder Duncan, but what it is like, in the long run, simply to *be* Macbeth. Yet, with all these allowances, there remains nevertheless a real difference of outlook between Spenser and Shakespeare. And it is such, I think, that only the neophyte will fail, in reading, to supplement the one with the other.

[1] Janet Spens, *Spenser's Faerie Queene* (1934), 123.

CHAPTER VII

BRITOMART'S DREAM

One image of good I have postponed, because it provides a transition to my next subject, the interaction of the Pageant element of the poem with the Romance of Chivalry. This image is Isis Church.

Up to the Seventh Canto, Book Five has shown us Artegall dispensing justice *simpliciter*. A pretty rough justice it is, too, enforced by the sanction of his horrible robot, the iron man Talus. Time and again we have been reminded that at the Cestus Tournament in Book Four Artegall bore on his shield the words SALUAGESSE SANS FINESSE, and that he was known as the Savage Knight. And from a formal point of view the book has also been crude, consisting, as it has, of the simplest of moral allegories. We are now to be shown that this is not enough, that such 'Justice' must be placed under the rule of a higher principle.

The canto begins with praise of Justice. Nothing on earth is more sacred, for it is the same virtue by which Jupiter 'containes his heavenly Commonwealth'. Next we are told that for this reason the ancients made Justice a god and called him Osiris 'With fayned colours shading a true case' (an important line, this, for any theory about Spenser's view of mythology). The wife of Osiris, however, is Isis; and she, as Spenser immediately explains, is an image of 'That part of Justice, which is Equity'—or, as a later stanza puts it, *clemence* (v, vii, 3, 22). Then we learn

that the male Osiris is a solar god, and the female Isis
lunar, so that the temple is named, oddly, after the lesser
light. The statue or idol of Isis is described in some detail.
The goddess, we notice, has one foot on a crocodile and
the other foot firmly on the ground,

> So meaning to suppresse both forged guile,
> And open force... (v, vii, 7)

There follows an account of the priests of the temple, much
of it drawn from the descriptions of Isis worship in
Heliodorus' *Aethiopica*. The priests' rule manifests what is
for Spenser Order of an unusual severity. They sleep on
the bare stone, are vowed to chastity, eat no flesh, and
drink no wine. Later in the canto, one of these priests
gives quite a different explanation of the crocodile from
the one we have had:

> For that same Crocodile *Osyris* is,
> That under *Isis* feete doth sleepe for ever:
> To shew that clemence oft in things amis,
> Restraines those sterne behests, and cruell doomes of his.
>
> (v, vii, 22)

But Spenser's first readers, I believe, would not have
objected to this as a contradiction. For a single emblem
might have many meanings. They would assume that
Spenser, having given the simpler one first, was now pro-
ceeding to the more inward.

But all Isis Church is seen through the eyes of Britomart. We have therefore to take into account where the
Isis Church episode comes in her story. Ever since the
Second Canto of Book Three we have known Britomart
to be passionately in love with Artegall, the Knight of

Justice, whom she first saw in a magic mirror made by
Merlin and kept in her father's room. Subsequently
Merlin has told her that she is destined to marry Artegall,
and by him to become ancestress of the British royal
house. At the tournament in the Fourth Book Britomart
and Artegall at last meet one another; but both are in
disguise. Britomart unhorses Artegall, and he leaves the
field early, before the adjudication, with what look very
like the sulks. In the Sixth Canto they meet again, by
chance. There is a fight, which finishes with Artegall
shearing off the ventail of Britomart's helmet and reveal-
ing her to be a beautiful woman. He falls in love with her
instantly; and though he does not dare to woo her 'so
suddenly' (IV, vi, 33), before the end of the canto they
have plighted their troth. And then of course they have
to separate, for Artegall has still to go on his quest. But
there is one incident in this eventful canto that has special
interest from the present point of view. I refer to the
forcible unveiling of Britomart, with its remarkable
accompaniment of numinous imagery. On seeing her
face Artegall fell on his knees 'and of his wonder made
religion' (St. 22). What is more, Scudamour too,

> when as he plaine descride
> That peerelesse paterne of Dame natures pride,
> And heavenly image of perfection,
> He blest himselfe, as one sore terrifide,
> And turning his feare to faint devotion,
> Did worship her as some celestiall vision. (IV, vi, 24)

The story is not resumed until the Sixth Canto of the
following book, when we find Britomart despairing of

Artegall's return. Talus arrives with bad news: Artegall is taken prisoner. Worse, he has been taken by the Amazon Radigund. Britomart sets off to rescue him and on her way comes to Isis Church. We return to the temple, therefore, but this time to look at it from Britomart's point of view.

Britomart enters the temple 'with great humility' (v, vii, 3); but Talus is not allowed in at all. Talus 'mote not be admitted to her part' because he belongs instead to Artegall's part, both of the book and of the virtue. Before the statue of Isis, Britomart prostrates herself on the ground
> and with right humble hart,
> Unto her selfe her silent prayers did impart.
>
>> To which the Idoll as it were inclining,
>> Her wand did move with amiable looke,
>> By outward shew her inward sence desining.
>>
>> (v, vii, 7–8)

'*Unto her selfe* her silent prayers.' Does this mean merely that she prays silently? Or is there also the suggestion that in praying to Isis Britomart is in some sense praying 'unto her selfe'? During the night Britomart sleeps under Isis' wings, and dreams that the statue is alive, first in conflict, but later in sexual play and in childbirth.

On the naturalistic level, the motives of the dream are evident. If a girl lately separated from her lover is ardently longing for her wedding day (and wedding night), nothing is more probable than that she will have an erotic dream. And the dream will borrow its materials, naturally, from her surroundings—in this case, the vestments of the priests of Isis and the mysterious crocodile

beneath the idol's foot. At first Britomart dreams that
she herself is doing sacrifice, dressed like the priests:

> with Mitre on her hed,
> And linnen stole after those Priestes guize.

(v, vii, 13)

Then there is a second change of clothing:

> All sodainely she saw transfigured
> Her linnen stole to robe of scarlet red,
> And Moone-like Mitre to a Crowne of gold.   (*Ibid.*)

In other words, she is *becoming* the goddess Isis; for, as we
have just learnt, the statue of Isis had such a crown
'To shew that she had powre in things divine' (St. 6). The
experience of deification, it seems, is one of great felicity;
Britomart 'joyed' at her transformation. Next, a tempest
rises and blows embers from the altar fire over the floor, so
that the temple starts to burn. At this the crocodile awakes
and eats up both fire and tempest, but then, having become
swollen with pride, he threatens to eat the goddess too.
She beats him back with her rod, whereupon he grows
meek:

> Him selfe before her feete he lowly threw,
> And gan for grace and love of her to seeke:
> Which she accepting, he so neare her drew,
> That of his game she soone enwombed grew,
> And forth did bring a Lion of great might.

(v, vii, 16)

The 'she' who brings forth the lion is left indeterminate:
is it Isis or Britomart? But this is perhaps a question
without much meaning.

On another level, the dream can be regarded as having
a more general bearing on the story of Britomart—as
belonging to the dynastic-epic aspect of the poem. From

Britomart's account of her dream, indeed, the priest of Isis is at once able to recognize her identity and lineage. Looked at in this way, the dream will be seen as reassurance for Britomart. It is a reminder, both for her and for us, that her marriage is of importance to all Britain. This the priest explains to her. The gods have sent her the dream to reveal 'the long event' of her love: the crocodile represents Artegall, and the lion means that she will bear him a heroic son.

But in the priest's explanation of the dream I think there also lurks something intended for us, something that Britomart is not shown. In v, vii, 22 the priest, having identified the crocodile as Artegall, adds that

> that same Crocodile *Osyris* is,
> That under *Isis* feete doth sleepe for ever:
> To shew that clemence oft in things amis,
> Restraines those sterne behests, and cruell doomes of his.

Therefore Artegall is Osiris; which makes good sense, since, as we already know, Osiris is Justice. But in so far as Artegall is Osiris, Britomart is also Isis. It follows that Britomart in some sense has her foot on Artegall's head, ruling him. Notice how at this point the dream interlocks with other episodes in their story. For we have already been shown Britomart defeating Artegall in the tournament and Artegall kneeling humbly before her in worship;[1] and in the latter part of the Seventh Canto we are to see her rescue him from the Amazon Radigund. In other words, Artegall is in his right place only when he

---

[1] And he himselfe long gazing thereupon,
At last fell humbly downe upon his knee,
And of his wonder made religion.   (IV, vi, 22)

is guided, even ruled, by Britomart. Without her he is ugly, *Saluagesse sans finesse*.[1] With her, a complex relationship is set up. For in the outer world he will be her lord and she an obedient wife; but in the very temple of Justice he will be under her feet, with Talus quite excluded. Outwardly Justice rules; in secret Equity. What is more, within the *sanctum* the two mingle in 'game'—yet another instance of opposites coinciding *in natura uniali*. There, beyond the world that the characters live in, Justice and Mercy unite and become one.[2]

At first sight the subordination of Artegall to Britomart seems to present a problem. Surely it runs counter to the ideal, set out in the previous book, of womanly submission, of 'soft *Silence*, and submisse *Obedience*' (IV, x, 51)? We may even feel inclined to ask whether it does not upset Spenser's whole hierarchy; for here we have the moon above the sun, the wife above the husband. But on reflection we recall that Spenser would be very familiar with the use of the inverted relationship in images of cosmic order. Think, for example, of all the Renaissance pictures of Mars conquered by Venus, disarmed by Venus, bound by Venus. Spenser would know very well that such images of female domination were meant to show Harmony and Reconciliation, or Beauty taming War and Strength and Wrath. The example is an apposite

[1] Artegall's *impresa* is possibly to be regarded as a rebus: SA LUA GESSE with SAGESSE (Fr., 'finesse') taken away—i.e. LUA. In mythology *Lua* was the name of a goddess of purification but also of destruction, to whom (together with Mars and Minerva) captured arms were anciently burnt; see Livy XLV, xxxiii, 2. Servius (*Aen.* iii, 139) identifies her with Diana.—F.

[2] Cf. Ps. lxxxv. 10: 'Mercy and truth are met together; righteousness and peace have kissed each other.'

Britomart's Dream

one; for Britomart herself is more a chaste Venus than a chaste Diana.

It will soon be apparent that no hierarchy we care about is impaired at Isis Church, if the episode is set beside that of Radigund, where a real breach of hierarchy occurs. For not only is Britomart's character in complete contrast to Radigund's, but also her relationship with Artegall is in contrast to Radigund's relationship with him.

There is nothing of the virago or feminist about Britomart. True, she has temporarily taken the role of a knight errant. But she became one only in order to find her lover; her outlook has always been entirely feminine. When she looks in her father's magic mirror to see if it will show her future husband, for example, the action is presented as the ordinary action of a normal woman. She looks not because she is in love, nor because she is wanton, but simply 'as maydens use to done'—as girls do. She 'wist her life at last must lincke in that same knot' (III, ii, 23). Radigund, on the contrary, is a real feminist. The motive of her aggression is explained to be revenge: she is revenging herself on all mankind because one man Bello-dant rejected her love (v, iv, 30). And her vengeance takes the form of directly reversing the roles of the sexes:

> For all those Knights, the which by force or guile
>   She doth subdue, she fowly doth entreate.[1]
>   First she doth them of warlike armes despoile,
>   And cloth in womens weedes: And then with threat
>   Doth them compell to worke, to earne their meat,
>   To spin, to card, to sew, to wash, to wring.

[1] Treat.

(v, iv, 31)

Can the humour here be intentional? I think it is. Radigund is to Spenser both a horrible and a grotesquely comic figure. Thus, when Artegall first saw her Amazons, they were 'an uncouth sight' (St. 21). Less obviously, when Radigund first saw him 'Her heart for rage did grate, and teeth did grin' (St. 37). Is this response not exaggerated almost to the point of burlesque? The burlesque later becomes indisputable:

> he raught her
> Such an huge stroke, that it of sence distraught her:
> And had she not it warded warily,
> It had depriv'd her mother of a daughter.   (v, iv, 41)

Yet there is nothing light-hearted in the portrayal of Radigund. She is too dangerous and too spiteful—

> And beare with you both wine and juncates[1] fit,
> And bid him eate, henceforth he oft shall hungry sit.
> (v, iv, 49)

There is also a contrast between Artegall's relations with the two women. Britomart he first encounters under the rules of the tournament, Radigund in a disorderly skirmish. When he does enter into an ordered relationship with Radigund, he begins by committing the fatal *hamartia* of agreeing to fight on her terms (Sts. 49–51). The terms are that the vanquished shall become the victor's slave: in other words, it is a struggle for unconditional sovereignty or 'maistry'. There follows a single combat that is very like, and yet also very unlike, the one with Britomart. Both end with Artegall un-

---

[1] Delicacies, sweetmeats.

covering his enemy's face and dropping his sword from powerless fingers; but the subsequent events are in sharp contrast. When Artegall sees Britomart's face he is overcome by love and humbly kneels to beg forgiveness. At first she is all for continuing the fight: she warns him to get up or she will strike (though she does not carry out this threat). Then Glauce intervenes and reconciliation follows (IV, vi, 19–30). With Radigund it is quite another story. Artegall strikes her to the ground and unlaces her helmet to kill her; but pity, 'ruth of beauty', makes him throw away his sword. Now Radigund revives and seeing her opponent unarmed renews her 'cruelnesse'. She lays on him with redoubled strokes; and the more he begs her to stop the more merciless she becomes. Defending himself with his shield, he offers to yield if she will stop hitting him. But even this is not enough: he must deliver up his shield and submit to her mercy. And then he is bound by his foolish oath:

> So was he overcome, not overcome,
> But to her yeelded of his owne accord;
> Yet was he justly damned by the doome
> Of his owne mouth, that spake so warelesse word,
> To be her thrall... (v, v, 17)

Radigund has him dressed as a woman and set to spin: 'So hard it is to be a womans slave' (St. 23). Here woman has usurped man's place in the hierarchy and man has abdicated it.

Whereas Radigund consciously designs an empire over men (and in the long run fails in her unreal design), Britomart's power, though real, is entirely unconscious.

In her role as Isis she enacts her sovereignty over Artegall-Osiris quite without knowing it—and without his knowing it. Nothing, in fact, is further from her mind. For she remains throughout a natural, even a naïve, girl in love. Notice how the interweaving of romance and allegory can give rise to a touching irony. We are made poignantly aware of the disparity between what Britomart and Artegall really count for in the universe, and their own ideas of their adventures. For of course the characters cannot know that they are in an allegory. We know it; but our knowledge is, in relation to their world, transcendent. They have a creaturely ignorance. With exquisite innocence—or with fatal blindness—they know not what they do.

A similar instance of this kind of irony comes near the beginning of the story of Una and St George. Una, deserted by St George, yet pitied by a beast of the field, complains:

> But he my Lyon, and my noble Lord,
> How does he find in cruell hart to hate
> Her that him lov'd, and ever most adord,
> As the God of my life? why hath he me abhord? (i, iii, 7)

These lines are strong anyhow. But they become much more so when you recall that the last is made up out of two places in the Psalms:

in the night-season did I sing of him, and made my prayer unto the God of my life. (xlii. 18)

Lord, why abhorrest thou my soul...? (lxxxviii. 14)

In fact, Spenser's humbled and forsaken woman addresses her false love almost as the Psalmist addresses God. What are we to make of this? The puzzle is not lessened by the next stanza, where we read:

> At last in close hart shutting up her paine,
> Arose the virgin borne of heavenly brood.

This last phrase is by no means mere decoration; for Una really does belong, as we know, to a higher order of being than St George. This is made clear in a variety of ways. Her father's kingdom, for example, is by rights the land

> Which *Phison* and *Euphrates* floweth by,
> And *Gehons* golden waves...   (I, vii, 43)

—Paradise, in fact, watered by the rivers of Gen. ii. 10–14.[1] (Hence the Well of Life and Tree of Life that restore St George during his fight with the Dragon.[2]) St George, however, is only of 'English race', descended

[1] 10. And a river went out of Eden to water the garden; and from thence it was parted, and became into four heads. 11. The name of the first is Pison: that is it which compasseth the whole land of Havilah, where there is gold; 12. And the gold of that land is good: there is bdellium and the onyx stone. 13. And the name of the second river is Gihon: the same is it that compasseth the whole land of Ethiopia. 14. And the name of the third river is Hiddekel: that is it which goeth toward the east of Assyria. And the fourth river is Euphrates.

[2] See I, xi, 29 and 46:

> It fortuned (as faire it then befell)
> Behind his backe unweeting, where he stood,
> Of auncient time there was a springing well,
> From which fast trickled forth a silver flood,
> Full of great vertues, and for med'cine good.
> Whylome, before that cursed Dragon got
> That happie land, and all with innocent blood
> Defyld those sacred waves, it rightly hot [was called]
> *The well of life*, ne yet his vertues had forgot.

> . . . .

> There grew a goodly tree him faire beside,
> Loaden with fruit and apples rosie red,

from Saxon kings.[1] At the House of Holiness he is in need
of Coelia's ministrations. But Coelia herself is comforted
by a visit from Una:

> when that fairest *Una* she beheld,
>   Whom well she knew to spring from heavenly race,
>   Her hart with joy unwonted inly sweld.
>
> And her embracing said, O happie earth,
>   Whereon thy innocent feet doe ever tread,
>   Most vertuous virgin borne of heavenly berth.
>
> (I, x, 8–9)

Una represents Truth in the allegory; and indeed she is
sometimes referred to simply as 'Truth':

> The guilefull great Enchaunter parts
>   The Redcrosse Knight from Truth...
>
> (Argument to I, ii)

> As they in pure vermilion had beene dide,
> Whereof great vertues over all were red [deemed];
> For happie life to all, which thereon fed,
> And life eke everlasting did befall:
> Great God it planted in that blessed sted
> With his almightie hand, and did it call
> *The tree of life*, the crime of our first fathers fall.

[1] See I, x, 60 and 65:

> And thou, faire ymp, sprong out from English race,
> How ever now accompted Elfins sonne
>
> . . . .
>
> For well I wote, thou springst from ancient race
>   Of *Saxon* kings, that have with mightie hand
>   And many bloudie battailes fought in place
>   High reard their royall throne in *Britane* land,
>   And vanquisht them, unable to withstand:
>   From thence a Faerie thee unweeting reft,
>   There as thou slepst in tender swadling band,
>   And her base Elfin brood there for thee left.
> Such men do Chaungelings call, so chaungd by Faeries theft.

> Forsaken Truth long seekes her love,
>   And makes the Lyon mylde...
>
> (Argument to I, iii)

St George, on the other hand, is never called Holiness. He is only 'The Patron of true Holinesse' (Argument to I, i). Throughout the book Una encourages, even rescues, him. And at one point she is associated very closely with divine Grace:

> Ay me, how many perils doe enfold
>   The righteous man, to make him daily fall?
>   Were not, that heavenly grace doth him uphold,
>   And stedfast truth acquite him out of all.
>   Her love is firme, her care continuall,
>   So oft as he through his owne foolish pride,
>   Or weaknesse is to sinfull bands made thrall:
>   Else should this *Redcrosse* knight in bands have dyde,
> For whose deliverance she this Prince doth thither guide.
>
> (I, viii, I)

Altogether Una seems to us numinous, while St George is never anything but natural.

But she does not feel it that way. In her own eyes she is simply a girl forsaken by her lover, her 'lord' and 'lion'. And she acts as if she needs him as desperately as he in fact needs her. This is particularly striking in her supposed reunion with St George at I, iii, 30:

> His lovely words her seemd due recompence
>   Of all her passed paines: one loving howre
>   For many yeares of sorrow can dispence:
>   A dram of sweet is worth a pound of sowre:
>   She has forgot, how many a wofull stowre[1]
>   For him she late endur'd; she speakes no more

---

[1] Time of stress, tribulation.

111

> Of past: true is, that true love hath no powre
> To looken backe; his eyes be fixt before.
> Before her stands her knight, for whom she toyld so sore.

Una's simplicity has here a quite touching irony. For we are aware that the knight she takes for St George is really Archimago in disguise.

Notice how fatal it would be to treat the figures in such an allegory as things to be translated—to say, in effect, 'Since Una equals Truth, let us substitute Truth for Una throughout. Let us stop speaking about her altogether, and speak about Truth instead.' For it is really the other way round. Truth and Grace are like Una. In *this* manner (Spenser implies), condescendingly like this, unwearyingly, humbly—as if it were they who needed us and not we who needed them—do the manifestations of divine Truth and Grace rescue and pursue us. We are reminded of the similar almost intolerable irony in Herbert's 'Love', where God himself appears as an inn-keeper,

> sweetly questioning
> If I lack'd any thing.

The stories in *The Faerie Queene*, then, far from being always 'encumbered by the allegory', may on the contrary gain an extreme poignancy from it. And they often convey an undercurrent suggestion that our own stories, in the world outside the poem, may have a similar irony and poignancy. But (at last we come to it) what of Spenser's stories themselves? Are they good enough, regarded simply as stories, to be worth our attention? This is a question of large enough importance to be worth a chapter of its own.

CHAPTER VIII

FACELESS KNIGHTS

Adverse criticism of the stories in *The Faerie Queene* is usually based on a false expectation. Both the complaints against 'faceless knights' and those against 'characters with no insides' come alike from readers who are looking for a novelistic interest. But it is quite wrong to approach the poem with this demand; for Spenser never meant to supply it. Occasionally, of course, he makes a very brief approach to the kind of fiction now valued in the novel: the conversation between the lovesick Britomart and her nurse, for example; or Una's 'reunion' with Archimago; or even, perhaps, the story of Malbecco (though that is more a fabliau or merry tale).[1] We should never concentrate, however, on passages such as these. It is always a great mistake to value a work of one kind for its occasional slight approximations to some other kind which happens to be preferred. If we can't learn to like a work of art for what it is, we had best give it up. There is no point in trying to twist it or force it into a form it was never meant to have. And certainly to read *The Faerie Queene* as a novel is perverse and unrewarding enough. It is like going to a Mozart opera just for the spoken bits.

The novel calls for characters with insides; but there are other kinds of narrative that do not. It is like the range of

[1] III, ii; I, iii (see above, p. 111); III, ix–x.

possibility we find in the visual arts. In a portrait we rightly expect character. On the other hand, to put elaborate portrait faces into Titian's *Bacchus and Ariadne*, or Botticelli's *Primavera*, or Tintoretto's *Mercury and the Graces*, would only spoil them. That the faces in these paintings have little character is not a fault but a quality, and a necessary quality at that. In literature, the narrative forms that do without character are quite numerous. They include, for example, the ballad, the Märchen, the adventure story, and the myth. Thus in the ballad *Edward*, all we know about the characters is that the mother is a murderess and Edward her penitent instrument: nothing else. In *Cinderella* the heroine is any and every, but no particular, lonely ill-treated child. In *King Solomon's Mines* the explorers are three brave men, just sufficiently distinguished by age and rank and profession for us not to mix them up. And in the myth of Orpheus and Eurydice (at least in the older versions), the hero is simply a great musician and a bereaved husband, and no more than that. Now, the chivalric romance, the kind of narrative that Spenser is writing, is another such form.

There is of course some range in the degree of character development possible in these narrative forms. And the range of possibility seems to be governed by an observable law: namely, that the more ordinary and probable the external story is, the more it should have fully studied characters. Obversely, the more phantasmagoric the external story, the less 'inside' its characters should have. Hence in Malory the early books of strange adventure are peopled with almost faceless knights, whereas in the final tragedy, as the events fall to this world, Launcelot and Guinevere develop more and more as characters. Hence, similarly, the utter ordinariness, even dullness, of the character of Gulliver, say, or of Alice, in contrast with the wonderlands of marvels they explore.

Nevertheless, all the forms of narration we are discussing will seem to lack character development as soon as they are compared with the novel. Now if character is undeveloped in them, what is their point? What do we go to them for? Certainly not for mere excitement, i.e. the alternate tension and relaxation of suspense and curiosity. If it were only for that, we would seldom re-read them. But when such stories are loved at all, they are re-read perhaps more than any others. Re-reading them is like going back to a fruit for its taste; to an air for...what? for *itself*; to a region for its whole atmosphere—to Donegal for its Donegality and London for its Londonness. It is notoriously difficult to put these tastes into words; and in a similar way the taste for a narrative 'world' is difficult to talk about. I suspect that all these difficulties may be put down to a single cause: the cause Mendelssohn had in mind when he wrote: 'The thoughts which are expressed to me by music that I love are not too indefinite to be put into words, but on the contrary too definite.'[1] For in a sense all words except proper names are general—too general ever to be exactly right. (Poetry can be thought of as the effort to heal this sickness in speech, this wound between language and reality. Significantly, all good poets love proper names.)

[1] Letter to Marc-André Souchay, 15 Oct. 1842; ed. Selden-Goth (1946), 314.

Thus, we go back to the close of *King Solomon's Mines* not for the excitement but for a sense of the *quality* of the danger; and this quality is something indefinable. To speak of the tons of rock between the treasure chamber and the outer world, of the Hall of the Dead with its petrified corpses all round you, and of the huge door of rock that nips and crushes Gagool, is only to make vague verbal gestures in its direction. Similarly, we can say that we go back to *The Wind in the Willows* for a sense of the sinister mounting unfriendliness of the Wild Wood, and of its sheer contrast with the homeliness of Badger's House. But to say that is to fail to communicate something in itself quite precise and definite.

A story of this kind is in a way more like a symphony than a novel. Corresponding to the themes of the musical form, the literary form has images, which may be delicious or threatening or cryptic or grotesque, but which are always richly expressive of mood. The images are in every possible relation of contrast, mutual support, development, variation, half-echo, and the like, just as the musical themes are. But the ostensible connection between them all—what keeps the meddling intellect quiet—is here provided by the fact that they are all *happening* to someone. They are all worked into the experience or the world of the characters 'whose' story it is. That, no more and no less, is the *raison d'être* of characters in the characterless story.[1]

[1] [A cancelled passage follows:] In Romantic lyric you may get such mood-images occurring separately, in simple isolation. There are quite a number of them, e.g., in Tennyson's 'The Palace of Art':

> One seem'd all dark and red—a tract of sand,
> And some one pacing there alone,

Faceless Knights

Of course, the character and psychology that are absent in one form may be present in another. For the images can be regarded as character-traits or drives within some super-character. Thus many of the images in *The Faerie Queene* can, if you wish, be identified with Jung's archetypes. St George and Prince Arthur readily fit the role of the Hero as Deliverer; the hermit in Book VI is a Wise Old Man; and Lucifera and the witch who created the False Florimell are Terrible Mothers. Similarly, the double role of Britomart as stern knight and lovesick girl is a symbol of the Persona. So is the illusory appearance of the False Florimell. And so, more obviously, is the brave façade of Braggadocchio the pseudo-knight. As for Amoret and the true Florimell, they can only be the Anima. But, even though all these identifications may be correct, certain cautions ought to be observed in making them. First, we should never forget that Spenser himself knew nothing of Jung's psychology. Secondly, the possibility should be kept uppermost in our minds that perhaps not all the characters of *The Faerie Queene* can be identified in this way, even though some can. Finally, we should be modest about the results of the identifications. For in any case it is always the symphonic treatment of the images that counts, the combination that makes out of them a poetic whole.

> Who paced for ever in a glimmering land,
> Lit with a low large moon.
>
> . . . .
>
> And one, a full-fed river winding slow
> By herds upon an endless plain,
> The ragged rims of thunder brooding low,
> With shadow-streaks of rain.

Connect such images with narrative, and you get something like Romance.

The Romance differs from the Novel in one very important respect, that it has no need to explain its images away. For its world is the world in which such images are native. With the novel it is very different. There each image has to be carefully accounted for in naturalistic terms and provided with its causal pedigree. In *Little Dorrit*, for example, the final horror of the whole nightmare in which Affery has been living comes when she creeps downstairs to see what her terrible husband Flintwinch is doing—and sees two Flintwinches, a waking Flintwinch and a sleeping Flintwinch, exactly alike. Since the story is a novel, this terrific image has of course to be explained away by some nonsense about a long-lost twin brother. In *The Faerie Queene*, on the other hand, duplication could actually be performed—as in fact it is, by the witch in III, viii, 5–8:

> In hand she boldly tooke
> To make another like the former Dame,
> Another *Florimell*...

> The substance, whereof she the bodie made,
> Was purest snow in massie mould congeald,
> Which she had gathered in a shadie glade
> Of the *Riphoean* hils, to her reveald
> By errant Sprights...

And in place of life, to rule the corpse she put

> A wicked Spright yfraught with fawning guile,
> And faire resemblance above all the rest,
> Which with the Prince of Darknesse fell somewhile,
> From heavens blisse...

This particular duplication will presently be loaded by the poet with entirely conscious allegories. But that is not a

necessary condition for the admittance of such impossi-
bilities to Romance. Even without it, Shakespeare
manages a not dissimilar effect. For when Troilus
witnesses Cressida's disloyalty, and exclaims 'this is
Diomed's Cressida...this is, and is not, Cressid',[1] it is
much more than a way of saying that such unfaithfulness
is not like her.

[1] *Troilus and Cressida*, v, ii, 134, 143.

CHAPTER IX

THE MISERY OF FLORIMELL

I

At the court of the Faerie Queen (that sweet golden clime) lived Florimell, who had long cherished an unrequited love for Marinell. One day she heard a rumour of his death. She took her white palfrey and set out to search through all the world until she found him alive or dead (III, v, 10). Riding through the forests she looked back, and saw that she was pursued:

a griesly Foster forth did rush,
Breathing out beastly lust her to defile.   (III, i, 17)

In terror she rode harder and harder. When she looked back again she saw that the forester was now a knight, who (as we know) meant her nothing but good—who was, in fact, the Rescuer *par excellence*. But nothing would allay her terror (III, iv, 48–51). She rode all that day and all that night until the palfrey failed (III, vii, 1–3).

Just as a lobster wears its skeleton outside, so the characters in Romance wear their character outside. For it is their story that is their character. Thus, Florimell is launched on this world by one desperate resolve. After that, all she does is to experience terror: first well-grounded terror, then groundless terror; but always terror, always gallop gallop gallop away.

Meanwhile we for our part know that the rumour that started her on her travels was a false one. For, in III, iv, we

have come with Britomart through the remotest lands
to the world's end, the sea-shore. There she alighted and
unhelmed for a breath of air (St. 7); a strange knight
galloped up saying in effect 'Get off that beach' (St. 14);
and she unhorsed him. But Britomart 'stayed not him
to lament'. Leaving him wounded badly in the side, she
rode on. She noticed—what was to her completely in-
explicable—that the strand was

> bestrowed all with rich aray
> Of pearles and pretious stones of great assay,
> And all the gravell mixt with golden owre;
> Whereat she wondred much, but would not stay.
>
> (III, iv, 18)

We stay, however, long enough to get the explanation.
It seems that the knight, Marinell, is the son of a nymph
Cymoent, who has persuaded her sea-god father Nereus
to throw him up all this treasure.

The mere image of the Rich Strond in itself accom-
plishes the work of Romance. The sea, however, is also a
lead; for we are now entering the most watery part of
The Faerie Queene. The mention of Proteus is also a lead
(he is to play an important part later in the book); but it
is much more than that. His prophecy, we can see, is
accomplished in Britomart's overthrow of Marinell.
Cymoent was warned to protect Marinell from women:

> For of a woman he should have much ill,
> A virgin strange and stout him should dismay, or kill.
>
> (III, iv, 25)

But only now is it obvious what this prophecy really
meant. The threat to Marinell is from Britomart and what

she stands for. Consequently, all Cymoent's life-long care
to keep Marinell away from girls has been wrong and
even contrary to nature. Like Florimell's quest—and
I think we are meant to notice this echoed irony—
Marinell's life has been based on a false premise. Marinell
himself is interesting as a character type not previously
encountered in the poem. He is the type of those who
reject love not vocationally, like Belphoebe, but pru-
dentially. He gives up sex because it is not safe. Finally,
this additional function of the story of Marinell should
be noticed, that it provides a narrative excuse for gliding
into the next movement of the poem.

For the news of Marinell's fall comes to Cymoent far
away,
>   whereas she playd
>   Amongst her watry sisters by a pond,
>   Gathering sweet daffadillyes. . .   (III, iv, 29)

And so we are able to have the wonderful passage of the
whole grief-stricken *cortège* riding over the obedient
waves in their chariots—'smooth chariots'—softly sliding
through the yielding water, drawn by dolphins 'swift as
swallows' leaving unbroken the surface behind them.
Everything listens to their lamentations. Even Neptune is
amazed at the sight, and feels compassion at the inex-
plicable sorrow of the nymphs. They, when they have
found Marinell alive, take him away, shearing through
the water, to Tryphon to be healed.

It is the contrast between this whole passage and the
violent encounter before that makes it so pleasing. From
sudden combat we glide through the image of the Rich

The Misery of Florimell

Strond into the soft pale liquid passage of the nymphs'
journey, with its satin sound and smoothness. In transi-
tions such as these Spenser excels.

2

Meanwhile Florimell staggers on on foot. At last

> Through the tops of the high trees she did descry
> A litle smoke...   (III, vii, 5)

This she takes to be a 'chearefull signe' of habitation, for
she is far from home and hopes for refuge and rest. But
in actual fact it is a sign of the greatest danger: it is smoke
from a witch's cottage. At first the witch is afraid of
Florimell (just as Abessa was of Una); then she is angry;
then for the time being compassionate. The witch's
lubberly son, however, again after initial fear and
amazement, begins a dangerous courtship. To escape him
Florimell gets up one morning before dawn and rides off,
going

> in perill, of each noyse affeard,
> And of each shade, that did it selfe present.

>   (III, vii, 19)

She is, of course, followed; this time by a monster like
a hyena, instructed by the witch to bring her back or
devour her beauty. Gallop gallop again. And now it is
Florimell's turn to come to the world's end. Far from
home like Britomart earlier in the book, she reaches the
'roring shore'. The continuation, however, is markedly
different. Britomart addressed the sea in lyrical medita-
tion, encountered Marinell, and rode on. But Florimell
sees a little fishing-boat, jumps on board, and pushes off,

abandoning herself to the mercy of the waves. Britomart could remain detached from the boat of her destiny and speak of it poetically as a 'feeble vessell' with a 'lewd Pilot' (III, iv, 9); but Florimell can only embark blindly.

The portrayal of Florimell thus seems limited to a series of merely external actions. Still, in Romance it is precisely the outward story that expresses inward life. Florimell's 'inside' is to be found outside, in the external events themselves. Indeed, her 'inside' *is* the story: the being lost, the being terrified, the being unable to interpret the world. Florimell is (as we say) 'all at sea'. And this misery becomes intensified. For the poem gets wetter and wetter, with the boat drifting out on the tide, and Fortune heaping on her 'new waves of weary wretchednesse' (III, viii, 20). *We* know that in actual fact Aeolus keeps his winds from disturbing the calm; but to Florimell it does not look like that. As it seems to her,

> farre in sea we bee,
> And the great waters gin apace to swell,
> That now no more we can the maine-land see.[1]

But before she can develop the point, she is involved in another adventure, the episode of the fisherman. This episode is in very deliberate contrast to the earlier part of the book. The poet exclaims:

[1] III, viii, 24. There is a similar irony, which also makes the sea ambivalent, in the final submarine canto of the Fourth Book. To Florimell it seems that 'greedy seas doe in the spoile of life delight' (IV, xii, 6). The poet, however, has only a few stanzas earlier given a very different view, speaking in his own person:

> So fertile be the flouds in generation,
> So huge their numbers, and so numberlesse their nation.
>
> Therefore the antique wisards well invented,
> That *Venus* of the fomy sea was bred.   (IV, xii, 1-2)

The Misery of Florimell

O ye brave knights, that boast this Ladies love,
Where be ye now, when she is nigh defild?

(III, viii, 27)

And indeed there is nothing of Fairyland here, still less
of Faerie form and courtesy. The fisherman, an earthy,
lecherous old rascal, is treated half comically. He wakes
up very alarmed, but at sight of Florimell he

      felt in his old courage[1] new delight
  To gin awake, and stirre his frozen spright:
  Tho[2] rudely askt her, how she thither came.

(III, viii, 23)

There follows an attempt at rape, which is handled with
some realism. Florimell's clothes get all spoiled with
'scales of fish, that all did fill' (St. 26).

Then Proteus intervenes, her apparent rescuer but in
truth (if she only knew it) the source of all her troubles.
He is the shepherd of the seas, and was out driving
Neptune's flock when he heard Florimell crying for help.
In a chariot drawn by seals he comes on the scene swiftly.
Though he is aged, with frost sprinkled on his head, he is
also vigorous. He administers ruthless punishment to the
fisherman, and finally casts him up on the shore. As for
Florimell,

  Her up betwixt his rugged hands he reard,
    And with his frory[3] lips full softly kist,
    Whiles the cold ysickles from his rough beard,
    Dropped adowne upon her yvorie brest.

(III, viii, 35)

[1] Heart; lust.   [2] Then.
[3] Frozen.

He takes her down to his sea-hollowed cave at the bottom of the sea. There he at first woos her sweetly with gifts and flattery. When that fails, he turns himself into a great variety of shapes (*c'est son métier*), to allure or terrify her. But when she continues obstinate he puts her in a submarine dungeon.

The curiously non-moral tone of this passage should be remarked. Proteus' conduct is both cruel and absurd, but Spenser passes no judgement on it. This may well be because an allegorical significance of Proteus precludes such a judgement. He is, I think, a personification of matter.[1] In the same way Florimell may (at least at this point) be the *anima semplicetta* come from the sweet golden clime into the sea of matter and the power of Proteus. Her imprisonment seems very like an allegory of the descent of the soul into material embodiment. If this is so, in the story of Florimell Spenser tells the story of every one of us, just as Blake does in that of Lyca 'conveyed To caves'.[2] But it should be emphasized that all this is only a momentary allegorical flash: the story as a whole is not allegory.[3]

3

The happy ending of the story of Florimell and Marinell is made to hang on the wedding of Thames and Medway held in Proteus' house. For Cymoent is a guest at the

[1] Proteus has a similar significance in Milton, *Paradise Lost*, iii, 600–5.

[2] 'The Little Girl Lost', in *Songs of Innocence*.

[3] Here I take a contrary view: the story of Florimell seems to me as allegorical as any in the poem.—F.

wedding, and she brings with her Marinell, now healed of his wound. Being half mortal, he is not allowed to attend the banquet of the gods. He takes the opportunity, therefore, of exploring Proteus' house; and of course he overhears Florimell crying in her dungeon. First he pities her. Then, when his heart is softened, he falls in love with her. But this makes him so ill that Cymoent has to take him back to Tryphon, and then to Apollo himself. Finally a correct diagnosis is made; Neptune is appealed to; and Proteus is forced to liberate Florimell.

But the spousals of Thames and Medway are not treated by Spenser merely as a part of the Florimell story, necessary to its plot but otherwise unimportant. On the contrary, they give an occasion for one of the greatest pageants in the poem. And it is even possible that this pageant was conceived long before the story it now belongs to. For as early as 1580 Spenser told Harvey that he planned an *Epithalamion Thamesis* in English hexameters.[1]

If we ask what this pageant is for, what the point of it is, the first answer must be that it did not have to have one. To an Elizabethan, a procession of mythological beings (all correctly described) would have needed no excuse. It was the sort of thing anyone would have liked. A point of which we should take particular note is that most of the rivers attending the spousals are English rivers. By turning these into deities, Spenser was doing for England (and for Ireland) what the ancient poets had already done for Greece and Italy. He was mythologizing

[1] See the first of the *Three proper, and wittie, familiar Letters* (1580); ed. Gottfried, p. 17.

—which is to say, civilizing—his country, just as they had mythologized theirs.[1]

The spousals also, however, have their place in the allegory of the poem. From this point of view they form the climax of a book on Friendship that is really a book on Reconciliation. This theme has had its most generalized expression in the previous canto, where Dame Concord made two young men shake hands:

> The one of them hight *Love*, the other *Hate*,
> *Hate* was the elder, *Love* the younger brother.
>
> (IV, x, 32)

Earlier, we have had the reconciliations of Cambell with Triamond in Canto iii; of Artegall with Britomart in vi; of Scudamour with Britomart in vi; of Timias with Belphoebe in viii; and of Placidas with Poeana in ix. And now Marinell too is reconciled, not only with Florimell but in a sense with all women. The parallel between the joining of two human destinies in love or friendship and the confluence of two rivers—risen far apart and far down stream united—would not have seemed to an Elizabethan a mere conceit. It was a deep analogy, firm enough to support a whole genre of river epithalamia.

A variety of other considerations may have contributed to Spenser's decision to introduce the spousals of Thames

[1] It is instructive to compare the spousals, from this point of view, with Drayton's *Polyolbion*. For it is clear from Drayton's address 'To the generall reader' that he had felt himself to be supplying a long-felt want of his countrymen, but that by the time the First Part of his poem was published, in 1612, he already noticed signs of a change in taste away from public and from mythological poetry. The change, however, was only a temporary one; later in the seventeenth century local poetry was again in great demand.

and Medway. Most simply there is his enduring love of rivers. Throughout his poetic life he found rivers, and fish, interesting in themselves. Next, there are the formal requirements of the poem. Spenser may have felt that for its balance it needs a watery scene at this point, to offset all the forest scenes earlier on. Earth has had its turn, especially in the Cave of Mammon; Fire has had its, at the House of Busyrane; and Air will have its, in the *Cantos of Mutabilitie*. But now it is the turn of Water. In the background, too, there is the speculation—both Paracelsus and Ficino entertained it—that aquatic elemental spirits may really exist (and who knows, perhaps in this as in so many things the ancients knew more than we). And in the foreground, finally, there is the idea that the sea is the home of Venus, that moisture is the prerequisite of generation. Only from the 'chaotic realm of change', only from 'that formless nature of which...every creature is composed' can Venus arise in her beauty.[1]

The catalogue within the epic is really a little art-form in itself, with its own laws and its own excellences. It had been a popular form when Homer enumerated the Achaean and the Trojan hosts (*Il.* ii, 484–877), and Virgil the Trojans and the Latins (*Aen.* vii, 641–817). It had recently been used by Tasso in describing the army of the crusaders (*Gerus. Lib.* i, 36–64). And Milton was still to find readers when he listed the devils obeying Satan's summons (*P.L.* i, 376–521). As it appears in all these writers, the epic catalogue is a pattern of proper names interspersed with descriptions, vignettes of place and

---

[1] Wind, *Pagan Mysteries*, 114, citing Pico.

person, and glimpses of legend, all arranged in the best order, i.e., with the greatest possible variety and balance. There should be a wide range of the eye into past times and distant places.

In the spousals of Thames and Medway, as in most epic catalogues, the names are, if you like, given: they are predetermined material. But the selection and the shaping are Spenser's. Thus, he begins with the great marine gods, Neptune, Amphitrite, Triton, and the rest, giving a good deal of pictorial description. Then come gods who were founders of nations; then Nereus, with the gods of famous rivers, such as Nile, Rhone, Pactolus, and Amazon. Here legends are worked in—Scamander is

> purpled yet with blood
> Of Greekes and Trojans

—as well as a topical bit about exploration in the New World. Next there is an interlude while Arion goes by playing on his harp, with the dolphin, still astonished, at his side. The English rivers follow, all clothed with emblems of their historical or commercial or aesthetic significance. None is a mere river: each is realized in terms of human values. Thus Thames himself wears the castellated crown of Troynovant; Dart is 'nigh chockt with sands of tinny mines'; Stoure is he that 'washeth Winbourne meades in season drye'; and Tyne's bank is the site of the Roman wall. The Irish rivers are more difficult to mythologize:

> I them all according their degree,
> Cannot recount, nor tell their hidden race,
> Nor read the salvage cuntreis, thorough which they
> pace.   (IV, xi, 40)

The Misery of Florimell

Then we have the bride Medua, elaborately described, and finally the sea-nymphs. With the nymphs we reach the extreme possibility of the epic catalogue form: a stretch of almost pure proper names, fifty of them. And yet, even here, how much more has been achieved by the poet's shaping hand! It is not just that the epithets are marvellously varied. The nymphs themselves have true mythological presence; for they unfold the separate qualities of womanhood we may suppose to be gathered in the bride they follow:

> White hand *Eunica*, proud *Dynamene*,
>   Joyous *Thalia*, goodly *Amphitrite*,
>   Lovely *Pasithee*, kinde *Eulimene*,
>   Light foote *Cymothoe*, and sweete *Melite*,
>   Fairest *Pherusa*, *Phao* lilly white,
>   Wondred *Agave*, *Poris*, and *Nesaea*,
>   With *Erato* that doth in love delite,
>   And *Panopae*, and wise *Protomedaea*,
> And snowy neckd *Doris*, and milkewhite *Galathaea*.
>
> (IV, xi, 49)

CHAPTER X

THE STORY OF ARTHUR

I

Closely interwoven with the story of Florimell is that of
Arthur. He is there when we first see Florimell as a
fleeing figure, before we know anything else about her:

> All suddenly out of the thickest brush,
>   Upon a milk-white Palfrey all alone,
>   A goodly Ladie did foreby them rush,
>   Whose face did seeme as cleare as Christall stone,
>   And eke through feare as white as whales bone:
>   Her garments all were wrought of beaten gold,
>   And all her steed with tinsell trappings shone,
>   Which fled so fast, that nothing mote him hold,
> And scarse them leasure gave, her passing to behold.
>
> Still as she fled, her eye she backward threw,
>   As fearing evill, that pursewd her fast;
>   And her faire yellow locks behind her flew.
>
> (III, i, 15–16)

This image, as we have seen, serves as the key-signature
of her story throughout the poem. It is first repeated at
III, iv, 46:

> Through thick and thin, through mountaines and through
>   plains,
>   Those two great champions did attonce pursew
>   The fearefull damzell, with incessant paines:
>   Who from them fled, as light-foot hare from vew
>   Of hunter swift, and sent of houndes trew.

The Story of Arthur

There it is Arthur himself who is in pursuit. Florimell's identity and whereabouts, we notice, are for Arthur attended by much uncertainty: 'at last of her far off he gained view', but night falls, so that 'her wayes he could no more descry'. And when he lies down to rest fancies present 'the sights of semblants vaine' (III, iv, 53–4).

It is on this occasion that we are told something of the greatest importance for the interpretation of Arthur's story:

> Oft did he wish, that Lady faire mote bee
> His Faery Queene, for whom he did complaine:
> Or that his Faery Queene were such, as shee:
> And ever hastie Night he blamed bitterlie.　(III, iv, 54)

Arthur is the figure in whom the Christianization of Paganism or the Paganization of Christianity—the poem's typical Renaissance syncretism—is most intense. At the literal level, in the fable, he is a knight endlessly seeking a Faerie mistress whom he has enjoyed in a dream. Or was it a dream, when he found the grass pressed down (I, ix, 15) where she had lain? Arthur is, in fact, in the predicament of Shelley's Alastor. It is a characteristic Romance motif, and it is unmistakably erotic. The name of the Faerie mistress, however, is not characteristic of Romance; for she is called *Gloriana*, and glory is a religious concept. (She is not, remember, to be translated as Elizabeth, though Elizabeth can as a compliment be compared to her.)

This leads us on to the Platonic aspect of the poem. Platonically considered, Arthur is the purged philoso-phical soul, smitten with a spiritual *eros* for the One, the

First Fair, and trying like Plotinus to make the flight alone into the alone. When at III, iv, 54, he wishes that Florimell were his Faerie Queen (or that his Faerie Queen were like Florimell) Arthur is therefore not entirely on the wrong track. Indeed, he comes very near to voicing a prayer that sums up the whole tradition of affirmative theology; except that here the prayer 'This also is Thou, neither is this Thou'[1] passes into 'O that this were Thou, o that Thou were this'. Unless Arthur only means 'O that I were now really finding Thee', it is a dangerous sentiment (Spenser's one big blunder as a doctrinal poet is that he fails to emphasize the danger). But there is something like it in Plotinus:

Those to whom the divine *eros* is unknown may guess at it by the passions of earth, if they remember how great a joy the possession of a beloved person is, and also remember that these earthly beloveds are mortal and harmful and that our love of them is a wooing of images.[2]

There is also, however, a level of Christian meaning. Whatever Spenser may say in the Letter to Ralegh, Arthur, as the soul whose gaze is fixed beyond the world, is the knight of Faith. Everything makes this clear, down to the details of his accoutrements. His great weapon, for example, is not his sword but his shield, because in Ephesians the *miles christianus* is described as 'above all,

[1] On the significance and authorship of this prayer, which Charles Williams may have found in St Augustine, see Victor de Waal, 'The History of Doctrine', *Life of the Spirit*, xviii (1964), 533.

[2] *Enneads*, VI, ix, 9; Stephen Mackenna and B. S. Page translate as follows: 'Those to whom all this experience is strange may understand by way of our earthly longings and the joy we have in winning to what we most desire—remembering always that here what we love is perishable, hurtful, that our loving is of mimicries and turns awry because all was a mistake, our good was not here, this was not what we sought . . .'

taking the shield of faith' (Eph. vi. 16). In the same way
Arthur keeps the shield veiled, uncovering it only

> when as monsters huge he would dismay,
> Or daunt unequall armies of his foes[1]

—recalling Hebrews xi. 34, where we are reminded that
through faith believers have 'turned to flight the armies
of the aliens'. Moreover, Arthur is the rescuer *par
excellence*, who saves others when all their own efforts
have failed. Champions of virtues, the knights of Holiness, Temperance, and Chastity, not to speak of lesser
characters, seem irredeemably lost, until they are
rescued by him. He is the 'prince of grace', it seems, in a
more than chivalric sense. Clearly some close relation
obtains between rescuer and redeemer, between Arthur
and a liberating faith in the person of Christ. Any direct
leap from the literal Arthur to the theological would of
course have horrified Christian feeling. But the Platonic
level provided a meeting-ground between. It was un-
objectionable to present an Arthur with philosophical
overtones, and the Platonic Arthur was in turn easily
syncretized with the Christian.

In any case, even Gloriana is herself, in the last resort,
merely an *image* of the One. She is adored, as Guyon tells
us, 'with sacred reverence', but not as God, only 'as
th'Idole of her makers great magnificence' (II, ii, 41).
Thus we are perhaps to think of a whole hierarchy of
emanations. Just as Gloriana is an image of the One, so
Florimell is an image of Gloriana. And just as Florimell

[1] I, vii, 34. An accidental unveiling of the shield is sufficient to defeat
Orgoglio at I, viii, 19.

is an image of Gloriana, so (passing into another story) the false Florimell is an image of the true. It will be noticed that in the most distant imitation the moral resemblance to the Original is very faint. The false Florimell is, as we say, evil. Yet in some respects the resemblance is still close enough to delude. When Sir Ferraugh seizes the snowy Florimell from Braggadocchio he takes her for the true Florimell, an illusion that she fosters and 'so made him thinke him selfe in heaven, that was in hell' (III, viii, 19). Similarly, when Sir Blandamour courts her, her slightest favours put him in a trance:

> He seemed brought to bed in Paradise,
> And prov'd himselfe most foole, in what he seem'd most
>   wise.   (IV, ii, 9)

And at the beauty contest after the Cestus Tournament, everyone but Britomart was ravished with wonder at the false Florimell,

> And weend no mortall creature she should bee,
> But some celestiall shape, that flesh did beare.
>   (IV, v, 14)

They all 'thought that Florimell was not so faire as shee':

> As guilefull Goldsmith that by secret skill,
>   With golden foyle doth finely over spred
>   Some baser metall, which commend he will
>   Unto the vulgar for good gold insted,
>   He much more goodly glosse thereon doth shed,
>   To hide his falshood, then if it were trew:
>   So hard, this Idole was to be ared,
>   That *Florimell* her selfe in all mens vew
> She seem'd to passe: so forged things do fairest shew.
>   (IV, v, 15)

It follows from the foregoing, if it is anywhere near the truth, that the Letter to Ralegh printed with the First Part of *The Faerie Queene* in 1590 gives a most misleading account of the poem. One feels like answering the Letter in such terms as the following:

'You say *I chose the historye of king Arthure*. But you didn't. There is no Uther in your poem, no Mordred, no Guinevere, no Launcelot, no wars with the Saxons. It was not the history of Arthur you chose, but the bare name. Or take your invoking of the precedents of Homer, Virgil, and Tasso. This implies that *The Faerie Queene* is an epic. But it isn't. An epic represents some great event that made a change in the world historically, whereas your poem, while it is full of events of a kind, is in another sense motionless. Fairyland as you have imaged it is "eterne in mutabilitie", since the sort of adventures that go on there are always going on. It is a presentation not of any change but of the enduring nature of man's universe. In such a poetic world there will be no real decisive event until it can be said that "*Natur's* selfe did vanish, whither no man wist".

'As for the structural scheme you profess to have followed, it is equally remote from your actual performance. *I labour to pourtraict in Arthure...the image of a brave knight, perfected in the twelve private morall vertues, as Aristotle hath devised*—yet already in the First Part of your poem you have introduced Holiness and Chastity, which Aristotle would never have dreamed of including among

Spenser's Images of Life

his virtues. *In the person of Prince Arthure I sette forth magnificence in particular, which vertue...according to Aristotle ...is the perfection of all the rest, and conteineth in it them all.* But that is not what you set forth at all. Certainly there is no trait of *megaloprepeia* (Magnificence) in his character, no slightest indication that he is a large spender. But there is probably a confusion of terms here, due to some bad Latin translation you were using. What you mean is Magnanimity, not Magnificence; *megalopsychia*, not *megaloprepeia*.[1] The crown of all the virtues is for Aristotle a right Pride or Magnanimity, which deserves and claims the highest honour. Now it is true that Alma shows the spring of Arthur's action to be Prays-desire (II, ix, 36-9). But even so, he has only as much resemblance to the Aristotelian *megalopsychos* as any good knight was bound to have.

'Finally, even the plot-summaries in your letter are contradicted by the text of your poem. For example, according to your Letter *The second day ther came in a Palmer bearing an Infant with bloody hands, whose Parents he complained to have bene slayn by an Enchaunteresse called Acrasia: and therfore craved of the Faery Queene, to appoint him some knight, to performe that adventure, which being assigned to Sir Guyon, he presently went forth with that same Palmer.* But in your poem Guyon and the Palmer are well started on their mission against Acrasia before they come across the babe with bloody hands.'

What, then, has happened? How did Spenser come to

[1] *Megaloprepeia* is defined by Aristotle in Nicomachean Ethics at 1122ª 19 ff., *megalopsychia* at 1123ª 35 ff. For the subsequent history of the latter term, see R. A. Gauthier, O.P., *Magnanimité: l'idéal de la grandeur dans la philosophie païenne et dans la théologie chrétienne*, Bibliothèque Thomiste, xxviii (Paris, 1951).—F.

write such a very careless blurb? Is it, perhaps, a correct but out-of-date description? Or are we wrong to assume that Spenser himself ever wrote it?

It is possible to imagine Spenser writing the Letter, I think, if we also imagine someone like Harvey at his elbow—someone trying to make the poem sound far more classical than it really is. Spenser will yield to the suggestion in a sense honestly, because he himself has no full understanding of what he is really doing. For his poetry is born out of deep brooding on his own experience and on the wisdom of the philosophers and poets and iconographers. It depends for its success on his obedience to the images that rise out of that brooding; and in that obedience he is a master. But wake him up—force him out into the 'literary world', a world buzzing with endless talk about Kinds and about Rules for Epic—and he is a child. He will accept almost any account of his work that a friendly Gigadibs suggests to him. But that will make no difference to what he *does* when he resumes his seat on the tripod.

A similar consideration to be kept in mind is this, that many of the correspondences in *The Faerie Queene* between passages thousands of lines apart are not consciously contrived at all. If they were, they would imply a sort of conscious intellectual labour of which hardly anyone would be capable, least of all Spenser. But in fact the correspondences have just the reverse implication. They show the extent to which he left the images alone to manifest their own unity, a unity far more subtle than conscious contrivance could ever have achieved.

However this may be, the account of the poem given in the Letter to Ralegh is demonstrably untrue, not only as regards its separate individual statements, but also in its whole tenor. For the poem is not an epic. It is rather a pageant of the universe, or of Nature, as Spenser saw it. The vision is a religious but not a mystical one. For the poet's basic religion, the religion that underlies the forms of his imagination, is simply the worship of 'the glad Creator'. Beyond that, perhaps, he was not much inclined to go. As he himself wrote, 'Lyttle have I to saie of relidgion...my self have not bene much conversant in that callinge.'[1] Yet, within this limitation, how much *The Faerie Queene* is able to contain ! For the world of the poem is changing every moment—'sprinkled with such sweet variety'[2]—through innumerable shapes, yet ever harmonious in its diversity: dangerous, cryptic, its every detail loaded with unguessed meaning, its parts so interlocked that you can hardly take them apart. It is, as we say, a comment on life. But it is still more a celebration of life: of order, fertility, spontaneity, and jocundity. It is, if you like, Spenser's Hymn to Life. Perhaps this is why *The Faerie Queene* never loses a reader it has once gained. (For that is one of the first critical facts about the poem.) Once you have become an inhabitant of its world, being tired of it is like being tired of London, or of life.

[1] *A View of the Present State of Ireland*, ed. Renwick, 109.
[2] VI, Proem, 1.

INDEX

Index

Index

Index